1001
VOCABULARY
AND SPELLING
QUESTIONS

1001

VOCABULARY
AND SPELLING
QUESTIONS

Printed in the United States of America

9 8 7 6 5 4 3 2 1

First Edition

For Further Information

For information on LearningExpress, other LearningExpress products, or bulk sales, please write to us at:

LearningExpress™

900 Broadway

Suite 604

New York, NY 10003

LearningExpress is an affiliated company of Random House, Inc.

Visit LearningExpress on the World Wide Web at www.learnx.com.

SKILL BUILDERS PRACTICE TITLES ARE THE PERFECT COMPANIONS TO OUR SKILL BUILDERS BOOKS.

Reading Comprehension Success	ISBN 1–57685–126–5
Vocabulary and Spelling Success	ISBN 1–57685–127–3
Reasoning Skills Success	ISBN 1–57685–116–8
Writing Skills Success	ISBN 1–57685–128–1
Practical Math Success	ISBN 1–57685–129–X

What people are saying about LearningExpress *Skill Builders*...

"Works perfectly! ...an excellent program for preparing students for success on the new Regent's Exam. I love the format, as well as the tips on active reading and study skills. And the pre- and post-tests help me in assessing my class' reading abilities."
> —Betty Hodge, 11th Grade English Teacher, Lancaster High School, NY

"The book provides help—help with understanding—for learners seeking to increase their vocabularies and improve their spelling."
> —Rose C. Lobat, Jewish Community Center of Staten Island, NY

"I love this book! It is easy to use and extremely user-friendly, and the end results are outstanding."
> —Janelle Mason

"If you are still dangling your participles, watching your sentences run on, and feeling irregular about verbs, check out this book. Recommended for the school, workplace, or even home for handy reference."
> —Julie Pfeiffer, Middletown Public Library

"I used *Writing Skills Success* and *Practical Math Success* in my JTPA classes. They're excellent, concise tools and offered quick, precise ways to get the basics across."
> — R. Eddington, JTPA Program Director

TABLE OF CONTENTS

INTRODUCTION

This book—which can be used alone, along with other vocabulary and spelling builders of your choice, or in combination with the LearningExpress publication, *Vocabulary and Spelling Success in 20 Minutes a Day*—will give you practice dealing with synonyms, vocabulary in context, antonyms, and spelling. It is designed to be used by individuals working on their own and for teachers or tutors helping students to build their vocabulary and spelling skills. Practice on 1001 vocabulary and spelling questions should go a long way in alleviating word anxiety!

Maybe you're one of the millions of people who, as students in elementary or high school, never understood the necessity of having to look up word after word in the dictionary. Or maybe you were often confused by all of those spelling rules, and those *exceptions* to the spelling rules. Or perhaps you could never see a connection between mastering vocabulary or spelling and everyday life. If you fit into one of these groups, this book is for you.

First, know you are not alone. It is true that some people relate more easily than do others to written language, and it is also true that some people have a natural gift for learning new words and for spelling. And that's okay; we all have unique talents. Still, it's a fact that on most jobs today, good communication skills—including vocabulary and spelling—are essential. A good vocabulary increases your ability to understand reading material and to express yourself in speaking and in writing. In the same way, being a good speller will make it easier for others to understand what you are trying to say. Without a broad vocabulary, your ability to learn is limited. The good news is that vocabulary and spelling skills can be developed with practice.

Learn by doing. It's an old lesson, tried and true. And it's the tool this book is designed to give you. The 700 vocabulary questions and 301 spelling questions in this book will provide you with lots of practice. As you work through each set of questions, you'll be gaining a solid understanding of word usage and spelling rules. And all without memorizing! The purpose of this book is to help you improve your vocabulary and spelling skills through encouragement, not frustration.

An Overview

1001 Vocabulary and Spelling Questions is divided into four sections:

Section 1: Synonyms
Section 2: Vocabulary in Context
Section 3: Antonyms
Section 4: Spelling

Each section is subdivided into short sets of between ten and twenty-five questions each. The book is specifically organized to help you build confidence as you further develop your vocabulary and spelling skills. The 700 vocabulary questions begin with synonyms (words that have the same meaning), move to vocabulary in context (determining the meaning of a word as it is used in a sentence), and finish with antonyms (words that have the opposite meaning). The

book's last section, which consists of 301 spelling questions, starts with easy words, moves on to easily confused and commonly misspelled words, and ends with more difficult words.

How to Use This Book

Whether you're working alone or helping someone brush up on vocabulary and spelling, this book will give you the opportunity to practice, practice, practice.

WORKING ON YOUR OWN

If you are working alone to review the basics and prepare for a test in connection with a job or school, you will need a dictionary by your side. A good hardcover abridged dictionary has about 1,500 pages and more than 150,000 words. A paperback dictionary may work for spelling, but you'll want a good hardcover dictionary to use for checking vocabulary.

In addition to the dictionary, you'll probably want to use this book in combination with a basic vocabulary builder, a spelling text, or with *Vocabulary and Spelling Success in 20 Minutes a Day.* If you're fairly sure of your basic vocabulary and spelling skills, however, you can use *1001 Vocabulary and Spelling Questions* by itself.

Use the answer key at the end of the book not only to find out if you got the right answer, but also to learn how to tackle similar kinds of questions next time. Every vocabulary word is defined; every misspelled word is spelled correctly. Make sure you understand the answer explanations—usually by going back to the questions—before moving on to the next set. If a word is still unfamiliar or confusing, look it up in your dictionary and write down the definition.

TUTORING OTHERS

This book will work well in combination with almost any basic vocabulary builder or spelling text. You will probably find it most helpful first to give students a brief lesson on how to use a dictionary. Have them practice looking up words for meaning and for spelling and then have them spend the remainder of the session actually answering the questions in the sets. You will want to impress upon them the importance of learning by doing and of checking their answers and reading the explanations carefully. Make sure they know the meanings and spellings of all the words in a particular set of questions before you assign the next one. For the synonyms and antonyms, you may want to have students use each word in a sentence.

ADDITIONAL RESOURCES

If you want more than just questions to answer, if you would like to study from a vocabulary or spelling builder, you may want to buy or take out of the library one or more of the following books:

VOCABULARY BOOKS:

Vocabulary and Spelling Success in 20 Minutes a Day by Judith N. Meyers (LearningExpress)

How to Build a Better Vocabulary by Maxwell Nurnberg and Morris Rosenblum (Warner Books)

30 Days to a More Powerful Vocabulary by Wilfred John Funk, Norman Lewis (Pocket Books)

Merriam-Webster's Vocabulary Builder by Mary Wood Cornog (Merriam Webster)

21st Century Guide to Building Your Vocabulary by Elizabeth Read (Dell)

10 Minute Guide to Building Your Vocabulary by Ellen Lichtenstein (Arco)

601 Words You Need to Know to Pass Your Exam by Murray Bromberg, Julius Liebb (Barrons)

Basic Word List by Samuel C. Brownstein, Mitchel Weiner, Sharon Weiner Green (Barrons)

Vocabulary Cartoons: Building an Educated Vocabulary with Visual Mnemonics by Sam Burchers (New Monic Books)

SPELLING BOOKS:

Practical Spelling: The Bad Speller's Guide to Getting It Right Every Time by Anna Castley (LearningExpress)

Six Minutes a Day to Perfect Spelling by Harry Shefter (Pocket Books)

Better Spelling in 30 Minutes a Day by Robert W. Emery, Harry H. Crosby (Career)

Spelling 101 by Claudia Sorsby (St. Martin's)

303 Dumb Spelling Mistakes . . . and What You Can Do About Them by David Downing (National Textbook Company)

50,000 Words Divided and Spelled by Harry Sharp (New Win Publishing)

S·E·C·T·I·O·N

SYNONYMS

1

The following section consists of fourteen sets of vocabulary questions, all of which ask you to find a synonym for a given word or phrase. (A *synonym* is a word that means the same or nearly the same as another word.) In the first six sets you will practice finding synonyms for single words. You may notice that the words in each set get progressively more difficult.

In sets 7 through 10, you are given a phrase with an underlined word. Notice, however, that the answer choices all fit into this phrase. In other words, you must know the meaning of the underlined word in order to choose the correct synonym.

In Set 11, you will find synonyms that are set up in analogies. Sets 12 and 13 ask you to find the meaning of prefixes, suffixes, and root words. Each question consists of two words with the same word part underlined. These two words may help you to find the correct meaning of the underlined portion.

Each question in the last set of this section gives you two underlined words or phrases and asks you to find the word that means the same as both of them.

SET 1 (Answers begin on page 115.)

For each question, choose the synonym.

1. Which word means the same as
ENTHUSIASTIC?
   a. adamant
   b. available
   c. cheerful
   d. eager

2. Which word means the same as ADEQUATE?
   a. sufficient
   b. mediocre
   c. proficient
   d. average

3. Which word means the same as ECSTATIC?
   a. inconsistent
   b. positive
   c. wild
   d. thrilled

4. Which word means the same as AFFECT?
   a. accomplish
   b cause
   c. sicken
   d. influence

5. Which word means the same as
CONTINUOUS?
   a. intermittent
   b. adjacent
   c. uninterrupted
   d. contiguous

6. Which word means the same as COURTESY?
   a. civility
   b. congruity
   c. conviviality
   d. rudeness

7. Which word means the same as FRAIL?
   a. vivid
   b. delicate
   c. robust
   d. adaptable

8. Which word means the same as
RECUPERATE?
   a. mend
   b. endorse
   c. persist
   d. worsen

9. Which word means the same as SUFFICIENT?
   a. majestic
   b. scarce
   c. tranquil
   d. adequate

10. Which word means the same as
COMPOSURE?
   a. agitation
   b. poise
   c. liveliness
   d. stimulation

11. Which word means the same as ECCENTRIC?
   a. normal
   b. frugal
   c. peculiar
   d. selective

12. Which word means the same as COMMENDABLE?
   a. admirable
   b. accountable
   c. irresponsible
   d. noticeable

13. Which word means the same as PASSIVE?
   a. inactive
   b. emotional
   c. lively
   d. woeful

14. Which word means the same as VAST?
   a. attentive
   b. immense
   c. steady
   d. slight

15. Which word means the same as COMPLY?
   a. subdue
   b. entertain
   c. flatter
   d. obey

16. Which word means the same as WILL?
   a. resolve
   b. spite
   c. sanity
   d. idleness

17. Which word means the same as ENLIGHTEN?
   a. relocate
   b. confuse
   c. comply
   d. teach

18. Which word means the same as RIGOROUS?
   a. demanding
   b. tolerable
   c. lenient
   d. disorderly

19. Which word means the same as OBLIVIOUS?
   a. visible
   b. sinister
   c. conscious
   d. unaware

20. Which word means the same as VERIFY?
   a. disclose
   b. confirm
   c. refute
   d. unite

21. Which word means the same as RATIONAL?
   a. deliberate
   b. invalid
   c. prompt
   d. sound

SET 2 (Answers begin on page 117.)

For each question, choose the synonym.

22. Which word means the same as ERRONEOUS?
    a. digressive
    b. confused
    c. impenetrable
    d. incorrect

23. Which word means the same as GROTESQUE?
    a. extreme
    b. frenzied
    c. hideous
    d. typical

24. Which word means the same as GARBLED?
    a. lucid
    b. unintelligible
    c. devoured
    d. outrageous

25. Which word means the same as EXPOSE?
    a. relate
    b. develop
    c. reveal
    d. pretend

26. Which word means the same as COERCE?
    a. force
    b. permit
    c. waste
    d. deny

27. Which word means the same as ABRUPT?
    a. interrupt
    b. sudden
    c. extended
    d. corrupt

28. Which word means the same as APATHY?
    a. hostility
    b. depression
    c. indifference
    d. concern

29. Which word means the same as DESPAIR?
    a. mourning
    b. disregard
    c. hopelessness
    d. loneliness

30. Which word means the same as CONTEMP-TUOUS?
    a. respectful
    b. unique
    c. scornful
    d. insecure

31. Which word means the same as TOTE?
    a. acquire
    b. carry
    c. tremble
    d. abandon

32. Which word means the same as DISTINCT?
    a. satisfied
    b. frenzied
    c. uneasy
    d. separate

33. Which word means the same as FLAGRANT?
   a. secret
   b. worthless
   c. noble
   d. glaring

34. Which word means the same as ORATION?
   a. nuisance
   b. independence
   c. address
   d. length

35. Which word means the same as LIBEL?
   a. description
   b. praise
   c. destiny
   d. slander

36. Which word means the same as PHILAN-
   THROPY?
   a. selfishness
   b. fascination
   c. disrespect
   d. generosity

37. Which word means the same as PROXIMITY?
   a. distance
   b. agreement
   c. nearness
   d. intelligence

38. Which word means the same as NEGLIGIBLE?
   a. insignificant
   b. delicate
   c. meaningful
   d. illegible

39. Which word means the same as VIGILANT?
   a. nonchalant
   b. watchful
   c. righteous
   d. strenuous

40. Which word means the same as ASTUTE?
   a. perceptive
   b. inattentive
   c. stubborn
   d. elegant

41. Which word means the same as
   COLLABORATE?
   a. cooperate
   b. coordinate
   c. entice
   d. elaborate

42. Which word means the same as INSIPID?
   a. overbearing
   b. tasteless
   c. enticing
   d. elaborate

SET 3 (Answers begin on page 118.)

For each question, choose the word that has the same or nearly the same meaning as the capitalized word.

43. JOURNAL
    a. trip
    b. receipt
    c. diary
    d. list

44. OPPORTUNITY
    a. sensitivity
    b. arrogance
    c. chance
    d. reference

45. INVENT
    a. insert
    b. discover
    c. apply
    d. allow

46. SPHERE
    a. air
    b. spread
    c. globe
    d. enclosure

47. REFINE
    a. condone
    b. provide
    c. change
    d. purify

48. PLEDGE
    a. picture
    b. idea
    c. quote
    d. promise

49. GANGLY
    a. illegally
    b. closely
    c. ugly
    d. lanky

50. SAGE
    a. wise
    b. obnoxious
    c. conceited
    d. heartless

51. NAVIGATE
    a. search
    b. decide
    c. steer
    d. assist

52. DORMANT
    a. hidden
    b. slumbering
    c. rigid
    d. misplaced

53. BANISH
    a. exile
    b. decorate
    c. succumb
    d. encourage

54. TAILOR
    a. measure
    b. construct
    c. launder
    d. alter

55. YIELD
    a. merge
    b. relinquish
    c. destroy
    d. hinder

56. CROON
    a. swim
    b. vocalize
    c. stroke
    d. yell

57. ETERNAL
    a. timeless
    b. heavenly
    c. loving
    d. wealthy

58. HOSTEL
    a. turnstile
    b. cot
    c. trek
    d. inn

59. STOW
    a. pack
    b. curtsy
    c. fool
    d. trample

60. MESA
    a. brain
    b. plateau
    c. wagon
    d. dwelling

61. ADO
    a. idiom
    b. punishment
    c. cost
    d. fuss

62. INTIMATE
    a. frightening
    b. curious
    c. private
    d. characteristic

63. OBSCURE
    a. hidden
    b. obvious
    c. reckless
    d. subjective

64. CONSIDER
    a. promote
    b. require
    c. adjust
    d. deem

65. HUMIDIFY
    a. moisten
    b. warm
    c. gather
    d. spray

SET 4 (Answers begin on page 119.)

For each question, choose the word that has the same or nearly the same meaning as the capitalized word.

66. AROUSE
   a. inform
   b. abuse
   c. waken
   d. deceive

67. MALICIOUS
   a. spiteful
   b. changeable
   c. murderous
   d. dangerous

68. HARASS
   a. trick
   b. confuse
   c. betray
   d. humiliate

69. FORTIFIED
   a. reinforced
   b. altered
   c. disputed
   d. developed

70. DELEGATE
   a. analyze
   b. respect
   c. criticize
   d. assign

71. OBSOLETE
   a. current
   b. dedicated
   c. unnecessary
   d. outmoded

72. EXPANSIVE
   a. outgoing
   b. relaxed
   c. humorous
   d. grateful

73. ACCOUNTABLE
   a. applauded
   b. compensated
   c. responsible
   d. approached

74. PHILOSOPHY
   a. bias
   b. principle
   c. evidence
   d. process

75. CUSTOM
   a. purpose
   b. habit
   c. buyer
   d. role

76. HARBOR
   a. halter
   b. statement
   c. refuge
   d. garment

77. MUSE
   a. tune
   b. ponder
   c. encourage
   d. read

78. RELINQUISH
  a. abandon
  b. report
  c. commence
  d. abide

79. VESSEL
  a. container
  b. furniture
  c. garment
  d. branch

80. SUBMISSIVELY
  a. raucously
  b. obediently
  c. virtuously
  d. selfishly

81. PONDEROUS
  a. heavy
  b. thoughtful
  c. hearty
  d. generous

82. STOICALLY
  a. impassively
  b. loudly
  c. curiously
  d. intensely

83. HAGGARD
  a. handsome
  b. honest
  c. gaunt
  d. intense

84. DISPUTE
  a. debate
  b. release
  c. divide
  d. redeem

85. ENIGMA
  a. laughter
  b. mystery
  c. enclosure
  d. shadow

86. JOCULAR
  a. lenient
  b. strict
  c. powerful
  d. jolly

87. REBUKE
  a. scold
  b. deny
  c. distract
  d. protect

88. RENOWN
  a. attitude
  b. fame
  c. health
  d. strength

SET 5 (Answers begin on page 120.)

For each question, choose the word that has the same or nearly the same meaning as the capitalized word.

89. ROBUST
   a. eager
   b. rough
   c. old-fashioned
   d. vigorous

90. SITE
   a. location
   b. formation
   c. speech
   d. view

91. MUNDANE
   a. proper
   b. ordinary
   c. greedy
   d. murky

92. COMPENSATE
   a. help
   b. challenge
   c. defeat
   d. pay

93. REMISS
   a. recent
   b. false
   c. negligent
   d. broken

94. IMMINENTLY
   a. sturdily
   b. actually
   c. soon
   d. later

95. INORDINATELY
   a. excessively
   b. exclusively
   c. purposely
   d. hesitantly

96. DISHEVELED
   a. rumpled
   b. divorced
   c. marked
   d. dedicated

97. DISILLUSIONED
   a. disadvantageous
   b. distracted
   c. disappointed
   d. disarming

98. QUERY
   a. inspect
   b. quote
   c. succeed
   d. inquire

99. CLEMENCY
   a. competency
   b. certainty
   c. destiny
   d. mercy

100. ATTRIBUTE
a. quality
b. penalty
c. speech
d. admission

101. SUBDUE
a. conquer
b. complain
c. deny
d. respect

102. CONFER
a. confide
b. consult
c. refuse
d. promise

103. REPAST
a. meal
b. debt
c. book
d. goal

104. APATHETIC
a. pitiable
b. indifferent
c. suspicious
d. evasive

105. SURREPTITIOUS
a. expressive
b. secretive
c. emotional
d. artistic

106. ANIMATED
a. abbreviated
b. civil
c. secret
d. lively

107. AUGMENT
a. repeal
b. evaluate
c. expand
d. criticize

108. INCREDULOUS
a. fearful
b. outraged
c. inconsolable
d. disbelieving

109. VINDICTIVE
a. outrageous
b. insulting
c. spiteful
d. offensive

110. MENIAL
a. lowly
b. boring
c. dangerous
d. rewarding

111. PANACEA
a. cure
b. result
c. cause
d. necessity

SET 6 (Answers begin on page 121.)

For each question, choose the word that has the same or nearly the same meaning as the capitalized word.

112. GLIB
    a. angry
    b. insulting
    c. dishonest
    d. superficial

113. INTRICATE
    a. delicate
    b. costly
    c. prim
    d. complex

114. COGNIZANT
    a. conscious
    b. educated
    c. mystified
    d. confused

115. MEDIATE
    a. ponder
    b. interfere
    c. reconcile
    d. dissolve

116. CONCURRENT
    a. incidental
    b. simultaneous
    c. apprehensive
    d. substantial

117. INDUCE
    a. prompt
    b. withdraw
    c. presume
    d. represent

118. MANIPULATE
    a. simplify
    b. deplete
    c. nurture
    d. handle

119. SATURATE
    a. deprive
    b. construe
    c. soak
    d. verify

120. PROSCRIBE
    a. measure
    b. recommend
    c. detect
    d. forbid

121. REFRAIN
    a. desist
    b. secure
    c. glimpse
    d. persevere

122. DOMAIN
    a. entrance
    b. rebellion
    c. formation
    d. territory

123. ESCALATE
    a. intensify
    b. inaugurate
    c. justify
    d. terminate

124. URBANE
    a. foolish
    b. vulgar
    c. sophisticated
    d. sentimental

125. ENUMERATE
    a. pronounce
    b. count
    c. explain
    d. plead

126. PERTINACIOUS
    a. gloomy
    b. self-assured
    c. destructive
    d. stubborn

127. AVERSION
    a. harmony
    b. greed
    c. dislike
    d. weariness

128. VALIDATE
    a. confirm
    b. retrieve
    c. communicate
    d. appoint

129. ANTAGONIST
    a. comrade
    b. opponent
    c. master
    d. perfectionist

130. PERSEVERANCE
    a. unhappiness
    b. fame
    c. persistence
    d. humility

131. HOMOGENEOUS
    a. alike
    b. plain
    c. native
    d. dissimilar

132. RECLUSE
    a. prophet
    b. fool
    c. intellectual
    d. hermit

133. NEVERTHELESS
    a. consequently
    b. therefore
    c. however
    d. unfortunately

134. PLACID
    a. flabby
    b. peaceful
    c. wise
    d. obedient

SET 7 (Answers begin on page 122.)

Choose the word that means the same or nearly the same as the underlined word.

135. its <u>inferior</u> quality
   a. noted
   b. distinguished
   c. lower
   d. questionable

136. in a <u>curt</u> manner
   a. gruff
   b. careful
   c. devious
   d. calm

137. their <u>perilous</u> journey
   a. dangerous
   b. doubtful
   c. adventurous
   d. thrilling

138. the <u>precise</u> amount
   a. fair
   b. exact
   c. undetermined
   d. valuable

139. to <u>commence</u> the meeting
   a. begin
   b. leave
   c. disclose
   d. terminate

140. a <u>humble</u> person
   a. common
   b. tolerant
   c. conceited
   d. meek

141. a <u>jubilant</u> graduate
   a. charming
   b. joyful
   c. stubborn
   d. scholarly

142. created a <u>replica</u>
   a. portion
   b. masterpiece
   c. prompt
   d. copy

143. a <u>temperate</u> climate
   a. moderate
   b. harsh
   c. warm
   d. cold

144. a <u>destitute</u> family
   a. poor
   b. wise
   c. traveling
   d. large

145. the <u>agile</u> dancer
   a. proud
   b. nimble
   c. humble
   d. talented

146. acted <u>brazenly</u>
  a. boldly
  b. blissfully
  c. brutally
  d. broadly

147. the <u>unique</u> individual
  a. rigorous
  b. admirable
  c. unparalleled
  d. remarkable

148. the <u>prerequisite</u> number of items
  a. optional
  b. preferred
  c. advisable
  d. required

149. <u>alleviate</u> the pain
  a. ease
  b. tolerate
  c. stop
  d. intensify

150. <u>inundated</u> with requests
  a. provided
  b. bothered
  c. rewarded
  d. flooded

151. the <u>unanimous</u> decision
  a. uniform
  b. divided
  c. adamant
  d. clear-cut

152. the <u>proficient</u> worker
  a. inexperienced
  b. unequaled
  c. efficient
  d. skilled

153. <u>obstinately</u> refused
  a. repeatedly
  b. reluctantly
  c. angrily
  d. stubbornly

154. to <u>rectify</u> the situation
  a. correct
  b. forget
  c. alter
  d. abuse

155. the actor's <u>aspiration</u>
  a. award
  b. oration
  c. ambition
  d. role

156. one <u>facet</u> of the plan
  a. skill
  b. problem
  c. detail
  d. failure

SET 8 (Answers begin on page 123.)

Choose the word that means the same or nearly the same as the underlined word.

157. expedite the process
    a. accelerate
    b. evaluate
    c. reverse
    d. justify

158. reversal of fortune
    a. luck
    b. status
    c. action
    d. thought

159. to absolve a person
    a. convict
    b. accuse
    c. forgive
    d. exclude

160. to hoist the flag
    a. lower
    b. destroy
    c. salute
    d. raise

161. the predictable outcome
    a. worrisome
    b. unexpected
    c. unfavorable
    d. foreseeable

162. to shore up a house
    a. demolish
    b. renovate
    c. support
    d. remodel

163. simmering anger
    a. unacknowledged
    b. diminishing
    c. righteous
    d. seething

164. to initiate a campaign
    a. support
    b. begin
    c. sabotage
    d. run

165. ravenous hunger
    a. natural
    b. ungratified
    c. voracious
    d. satisfied

166. uninhabitable island
    a. deserted
    b. unlivable
    c. remote
    d. uncivilized

167. suppressed anger
    a. explosive
    b. repressed
    c. minimized
    d. expressed

168. to be <u>immersed in</u> study
   a. trapped in
   b. absorbed in
   c. learning through
   d. enriched by

169. <u>secular</u> music
   a. non-religious
   b. atheistic
   c. religious
   d. ancient

170. to <u>haggle</u> over the price
   a. bargain
   b. complain
   c. worry
   d. cheat

171. <u>palpable</u> tension
   a. rising
   b. understated
   c. nervous
   d. tangible

172. to get <u>a vicarious</u> thrill
   a. a dangerous
   b. a forbidden
   c. an imaginary
   d. a secretive

173. urban <u>sprawl</u>
   a. decay
   b. development
   c. haphazard growth
   d. increase in crime

174. an <u>exotic</u> land
   a. foreign and intriguing
   b. alien and frightening
   c. ludicrous and amusing
   d. remote and boring

175. a <u>meandering</u> stream
   a. clear
   b. flowing
   c. polluted
   d. winding

176. a <u>precarious</u> situation
   a. joyous
   b. dangerous
   c. unforgettable
   d. secure

177. a <u>precocious</u> child
   a. advanced
   b. bratty
   c. abused
   d. educated

178. to be in a <u>quandary</u>
   a. dilemma
   b. position
   c. mood
   d. trap

SET 9 (Answers begin on page 124.)

Choose the word that means the same or nearly the same as the underlined word.

179. to <u>cite</u> a source
    a. mention
    b. discredit
    c. prove
    d. plagiarize

180. an <u>insatiable</u> appetite
    a. declining
    b. unquenchable
    c. satisfied
    d. ample

181. a <u>nominal</u> sum
    a. insignificant
    b. agreed upon
    c. honest
    d. predetermined

182. an <u>inhibited</u> response
    a. heightened
    b. average
    c. restrained
    d. unanticipated

183. the <u>essence</u> of a book or film
    a. fundamental part
    b. summary
    c. worthwhile section
    d. original part

184. to delete an <u>expletive</u>
    a. redundant word
    b. biased section
    c. entire section
    d. obscene word

185. the <u>ripple</u> effect of inflation
    a. gradually spreading
    b. unfortunate
    c. adverse
    d. unpredictable

186. an initiation <u>rite</u>
    a. beginning
    b. ceremony
    c. disappointment
    d. risk

187. a political <u>maverick</u>
    a. hack
    b. criminal
    c. hero
    d. dissenter

188. to commit <u>mayhem</u>
    a. wanton destruction
    b. burglary
    c. manslaughter
    d. restitution

189. to <u>neutralize</u> an effect
    a. heighten
    b. precipitate
    c. maintain
    d. counteract

190. an economic <u>shackle</u>
  a. impetus to growth
  b. downturn
  c. restraint to further growth
  d. failing

191. to <u>censure</u> an official
  a. control
  b. elect
  c. criticize
  d. defeat

192. an <u>insufferable</u> snob
  a. intolerable
  b. complete
  c. pitiable
  d. superior

193. an intricate <u>labyrinth</u>
  a. snare
  b. maze
  c. prison
  d. network

194. the <u>quintessence</u> of evil
  a. very essence
  b. cessation
  c. cause
  d. theory

195. a <u>consummate</u> liar
  a. half
  b. revealed
  c. complete
  d. harmful

196. to <u>eclipse</u> another person
  a. destroy
  b. enrage
  c. overshadow
  d. elevate

197. his speech filled with <u>hyperbole</u>
  a. sincerity
  b. exaggeration
  c. understatement
  d. anger

198. the <u>proponent</u> of new laws
  a. advocate
  b. delinquent
  c. idealist
  d. critic

199. your <u>disparaging</u> remark
  a. encouraging
  b. final
  c. restricting
  d. belittling

200. to be <u>apprised of</u> the situation
  a. interrupted by
  b. bothered by
  c. changed by
  d. informed of

SET 10 (Answers begin on page 125.)

Choose the word that means the same or nearly the same as the underlined word.

201. to <u>scrutinize</u> the document
   a. handle
   b. examine
   c. neglect
   d. distribute

202. her <u>irrelevant</u> statement
   a. independent
   b. firm
   c. normal
   d. nonessential

203. our supervisor's <u>rigidity</u>
   a. misery
   b. viewpoint
   c. inflexibility
   d. disagreement

204. your <u>magnanimous</u> deed
   a. enormous
   b. scholarly
   c. generous
   d. dignified

205. <u>partisan</u> politics
   a. honorable
   b. neutral
   c. biased
   d. unlawful

206. <u>articulate</u> the philosophy
   a. trust
   b. refine
   c. verify
   d. express

207. his <u>meticulous</u> examination
   a. delicate
   b. painstaking
   c. responsible
   d. objective

208. his <u>animosity</u> toward us
   a. readiness
   b. compassion
   c. hostility
   d. impatience

209. write your <u>synopsis</u>
   a. summary
   b. chapter
   c. bibliography
   d. verification

210. the <u>meager</u> supply
   a. sincere
   b. abundant
   c. scant
   d. precise

211. a <u>noxious</u> odor
   a. floral
   b. pleasant
   c. harmful
   d. strange

212. to have <u>equity</u>
   a. justice
   b. certainty
   c. wealth
   d. dread

213. our neighbor's <u>affluence</u>
 a. disregard
 b. wealth
 c. greed
 d. shame

214. the <u>ominous</u> cloud
 a. ordinary
 b. motionless
 c. fluffy
 d. threatening

215. to <u>defray</u> the cost
 a. pay
 b. defend
 c. delay
 d. reduce

216. his <u>impromptu</u> speech
 a. boring
 b. memorable
 c. rehearsed
 d. spontaneous

217. voted against the new <u>statute</u>
 a. candidate
 b. law
 c. government
 d. board

218. his <u>spurious</u> statement
 a. prevalent
 b. false
 c. melancholy
 d. actual

219. to <u>emulate</u> another person
 a. imitate
 b. convince
 c. fascinate
 d. punish

220. her many <u>idiosyncrasies</u>
 a. mistakes
 b. eccentricities
 c. symptoms
 d. offenses

221. a <u>penurious</u> person
 a. indigent
 b. stingy
 c. self-righteous
 d. indignant

222. the gift of <u>precognition</u>
 a. talent
 b. insight
 c. clairvoyance
 d. intelligence

223. the <u>penumbra</u> of an eclipse
 a. very beginning
 b. partial shadow
 c. point of complete illumination
 d. point of complete shadow

224. a <u>circumspect</u> decision
 a. cowardly
 b. indirect
 c. careful
 d. wrong-headed

SET 11 (Answers begin on page 126.)

225. *Tactful* is to *diplomatic* as *bashful* is to
a. timid
b. confident
c. uncomfortable
d. bold

226. *Embarrassed* is to *humiliated* as *frightened* is to
a. terrified
b. agitated
c. courageous
d. reckless

227. *Control* is to *dominate* as *magnify* is to
a. enlarge
b. preserve
c. decrease
d. divide

228. *Exactly* is to *precisely* as *evidently* is to
a. positively
b. apparently
c. narrowly
d. unquestionably

229. *Neophyte* is to *novice* as *pursuit* is to
a. quest
b. restraint
c. passion
d. speed

230. *Regard* is to *esteem* as *ambivalence* is to
a. uncertainty
b. withdrawal
c. resemblance
d. injustice

231. *Restrain* is to *curb* as *recant* is to
a. foretell
b. retract
c. entertain
d. resent

232. *Capricious* is to *whimsical* as *shrewd* is to
a. cruel
b. different
c. grateful
d. astute

233. *Obstinate* is to *stubborn* as *staunch* is to
a. oppressive
b. ominous
c. faithful
d. arrogant

234. *Resolutely* is to *perseveringly* as *spuriously* is to
a. falsely
b. dejectedly
c. delightfully
d. abundantly

235. *Hypocrite* is to *phony* as *lethargy* is to
a. modesty
b. stupor
c. pride
d. disappointment

236. *Component* is to *constituent* as *epoch* is to
a. bliss
b. perjury
c. era
d. emotion

237. *Dupe* is to *deceive* as *exculpate* is to
a. falsify
b. disappear
c. invade
d. absolve

238. *Heterogeneous* is to *mixed* as *profuse* is to
a. lush
b. timid
c. scarce
d. painful

239. *Disclose* is to *reveal* as *imitate* is to
a. forbid
b. copy
c. announce
d. enlarge

240. *Conceal* is to *obscure* as *procrastinate* is to
a. anticipate
b. relinquish
c. delay
d. pretend

241. *Futilely* is to *vainly* as *covertly* is to
a. secretly
b. grandly
c. seductively
d. habitually

242. *Opposing* is to *differing* as *candid* is to
a. conclusive
b. strict
c. credible
d. frank

243. *Expeditiously* is to *swiftly* as *diligently* is to
a. openly
b. persistently
c. increasingly
d. vividly

SET 12 (Answers begin on page 127.)

Choose the word or phrase that means the same or nearly the same as the underlined prefix, suffix, or other word part.

244. care<u>ful</u> and hate<u>ful</u>
   a. empty of
   b. full of
   c. clear of
   d. reminded of

245. <u>un</u>holy and <u>un</u>coordinated
   a. same as
   b. related to
   c. besides
   d. opposite of

246. gentle<u>ness</u> and pretentious<u>ness</u>
   a. state or quality
   b. case or plight
   c. requirement or need
   d. care or attention

247. <u>re</u>build and <u>re</u>assign
   a. undo or cancel
   b. maintain or perpetuate
   c. destroy or consume
   d. again or anew

248. <u>semi</u>gloss and <u>semi</u>retired
   a. over or overly
   b. partial or partially
   c. by or beside
   d. separate or disunited

249. <u>sur</u>face and <u>sur</u>vive
   a. under or below
   b. between or among
   c. over or above
   d. across or beside

250. adult<u>hood</u> and neighbor<u>hood</u>
   a. spot, place, or site
   b. adjoin or border
   c. condition, state, or quality
   d. remove or transfer

251. <u>tri</u>cycle and <u>tri</u>angle
   a. straight line
   b. pyramid
   c. double
   d. three

252. love<u>ly</u> and lone<u>ly</u>
   a. opposite or contrasting
   b. like or resembling
   c. distinct or special
   d. intense or concentrated

253. <u>anti</u>trust and <u>anti</u>matter
   a. toward or near
   b. opposing or against
   c. impose or impress
   d. breach or disturb

254. <u>dis</u>enfranchise and <u>dis</u>mount
   a. undo
   b. redo
   c. overdo
   d. expunge

255. <u>inter</u>dependent and <u>inter</u>state
   a. alongside or beside
   b. present or current
   c. between or among
   d. under or beneath

256. <u>com</u>ponent and <u>com</u>mingle
   a. together
   b. apart
   c. not
   d. whole

257. suf<u>fix</u> and pre<u>fix</u>
   a. to reveal
   b. to limit
   c. to adapt
   d. to fasten

258. <u>pre</u>history and <u>pre</u>game
   a. later or after
   b. simultaneously or together
   c. before or prior to
   d. by or near

259. <u>super</u>intendent and <u>super</u>impose
   a. below or under
   b. adjacent or beside
   c. subsequent or after
   d. above or over

260. <u>ambi</u>valent and <u>ambi</u>dextrous
   a. neither
   b. some
   c. both
   d. after

261. <u>neo</u>phyte and <u>neo</u>realism
   a. old or past
   b. new or recent
   c. amateur or novice
   d. following or after

262. <u>per</u>vade and <u>per</u>verse
   a. meticulously, carefully
   b. completely, intensely
   c. separately, aloofly
   d. randomly, accidentally

263. <u>sub</u>jugate and <u>sub</u>human
   a. below, under
   b. above, over
   c. beside, tandem
   d. by, near

264. pro<u>pel</u> and im<u>pel</u>
   a. fall
   b. push
   c. run
   d. drag

265. <u>audi</u>tion and <u>audi</u>ence
   a. hear
   b. see
   c. hall
   d. trial

SET 13 (Answers begin on page 127.)

Choose the word or phrase that means the same or nearly the same as the underlined prefix, suffix, or other word part.

266. <u>psycho</u>therapy and <u>psycho</u>path
   a. disease, illness
   b. mind, mental
   c. nerves, vigor
   d. neurosis, complex

267. <u>omni</u>vorous and <u>omni</u>present
   a. foreign
   b. parallel
   c. all
   d. none

268. betray<u>al</u> and retriev<u>al</u>
   a. resembling
   b. lack of
   c. one who
   d. action or process of

269. child<u>ish</u> and wasp<u>ish</u>
   a. having the appearance of
   b. having the qualities of
   c. engaged in the act of
   d. mindful of

270. cheap<u>en</u> or redd<u>en</u>
   a. to cause to be or to become
   b. one who
   c. to act upon
   d. to come before

271. sleep<u>y</u> and weep<u>y</u>
   a. on top of
   b. regardless of
   c. tending toward
   d. contrasting to

272. <u>be</u>guile and <u>be</u>witched
   a. thoroughly
   b. haphazardly
   c. undone
   d. repeated

273. <u>aero</u>bics and <u>aero</u>dynamic
   a. water
   b. air
   c. earth
   d. fire

274. <u>mal</u>absorption and <u>mal</u>adroit
   a. not or nothing
   b. bad or abnormal
   c. want or need
   d. without or lacking

275. <u>hetero</u>geneous and <u>hetero</u>dox
   a. to or toward
   b. in or inside of
   c. like or same
   d. other or different

276. <u>photo</u>active and <u>photo</u>graph
   a. white
   b. imprint
   c. light
   d. picture

277. aquar<u>ium</u> and auditor<u>ium</u>
    a. place for
    b. state of being
    c. former
    d. the study of

278. <u>ex</u>communicate and <u>ex</u>cept
    a. open
    b. close to
    c. out of
    d. free of

279. <u>macro</u>cosm and <u>macro</u>scopic
    a. long
    b. heavy
    c. small
    d. large

280. abnormal<u>ity</u> and real<u>ity</u>
    a. same or equal
    b. state or quality
    c. single or only
    d. act or deed

281. <u>retro</u>rocket or <u>retro</u>active
    a. thrust or propel
    b. back or backward
    c. front or ahead
    d. slow or late

282. <u>poly</u>gamous or <u>poly</u>glot
    a. varied
    b. amount
    c. number
    d. many

283. dermat<u>ology</u> and astr<u>ology</u>
    a. science or study
    b. skill or talent
    c. hidden or obscure
    d. type or kind

284. dia<u>logue</u> or trave<u>logue</u>
    a. learning or discovery
    b. teaching or pedagogy
    c. speech or discourse
    d. urbane or elegant

285. aera<u>tion</u> or absorp<u>tion</u>
    a. process
    b. sequence
    c. condition
    d. pattern

286. <u>crypto</u>genic and <u>crypto</u>graphy
    a. written or inscribed
    b. hidden or secret
    c. cold or frozen
    d. silent or calm

287. <u>myo</u>tonic and <u>myo</u>cardial
    a. nerve
    b. skin
    c. muscle
    d. vein

SET 14 (Answers begin on page 128.)

Choose the word that means the same as both of the underlined words or phrases.

288. An animal and to trail or track persistently
   a. cat
   b. fish
   c. dog
   d. snail

289. a kind of bird and to brag or boast over a win
   a. curlew
   b. crow
   c. parrot
   d. hawk

290. a meadow and an area of expertise
   a. field
   b. plain
   c. tract
   d. pasture

291. a motion picture and a fine coating
   a. reel
   b. skin
   c. film
   d. flick

292. a device to prevent crying out and a joke
   a. kid
   b. prank
   c. gag
   d. choke

293. midway between extremes and a kind of psychic
   a. prescient
   b. cerebral
   c. seer
   d. medium

294. a game and a small body of water
   a. pool
   b. tarn
   c. puddle
   d. sport

295. middle and stingy
   a. close
   b. base
   c. mean
   d. petty

296. a child's toy and a moving device
   a. ball
   b. top
   c. cart
   d. dolly

297. quiet and a liquor-making device
   a. still
   b. grog
   c. rest
   d. hush

298. to swagger and a bar or rod used as a brace
   a. stride
   b. tread
   c. prance
   d. strut

299. a sudden increase and a part of a sailboat
   a. swell
   b. boom
   c. gust
   d. sail

300. swift and to abstain from food
   a. starve
   b. fleet
   c. fast
   d. famish

301. a musical instrument and a body part
   a. organ
   b. foot
   c. lute
   d. digit

302. a wooden structure and to rig criminal evidence
   a. shed
   b. frame
   c. stool
   d. bridge

303. firm or unyielding and a part of a ship
   a. head
   b. jib
   c. stern
   d. bow

304. a libertine and a yard and garden implement
   a. rake
   b. roué
   c. gear
   d. tool

305. a spicy dish and to gain favor by flattering
   a. salsa
   b. curry
   c. pesto
   d. relish

306. a kind of lurid magazine story and the soft, moist inside of fruit
   a. mash
   b. flesh
   c. skin
   d. pulp

S·E·C·T·I·O·N 2
VOCABULARY IN CONTEXT

The thirteen sets in the section will give you practice answering questions that ask you to find vocabulary in context. In Section 1 you had less information to help you choose the correct answer, but in this section each question will provide you with a sentence or a passage that will offer you "clues" to finding the appropriate word or phrase.

In the first five sets, you will choose the word the best fits the blank in a given sentence. Sets 20 and 21 ask you to choose from four dictionary definitions. In Sets 22 and 23, you will replace a common word or phrase with a more descriptive one. Finally, in the last four sets, your context clues will come in the form of both short and long passages.

SET 15 (Answers begin on page 129.)

Choose the word that best fills the blank in the following sentences.

307. The main _____ Jim had was too many parking tickets.
a. disaster
b. search
c. request
d. problem

308. While trying to _____ his pet iguana from a tree, Travis Stevens fell and broke his ankle.
a. examine
b. transfer
c. rescue
d. pardon

309. When I bought my fancy car, I didn't stop to _____ how I'd pay for it.
a. consider
b. promote
c. require
d. adjust

310. We knew nothing about Betty, because she was so _____.
a. expressive
b. secretive
c. emotional
d. artistic

311. We were tired when we reached the _____, but the spectacular view of the valley below was worth the hike.
a. circumference
b. summit
c. fulcrum
d. nadir

312. The _____ of not turning in your homework is after-school detention.
a. reward
b. denial
c. consequence
d. cause

313. His suit had a(n) _____ odor, as if it had been closed up for a long time in an old trunk.
a. aged
b. dried-up
c. musty
d. decrepit

314. Every day he had to deal with crowds of noisy, demanding people, so he longed most of all for _____.
a. solitude
b. association
c. loneliness
d. irrelevancy

315. I was blamed for the town's bad fortune, and so I was _____ by everyone.
a. regarded
b. shunned
c. neglected
d. forewarned

316. When Bobby Wilcox let a frog loose in class, Ms. Willy became so _____ that she threw an eraser.
a. animated
b. incautious
c. irate
d. irradiated

317. The star's _____ remarks about other actors he had worked with made the whole company careful about what they said in front of him.
a. spiteful
b. changeable
c. approving
d. prudent

318. The teacher put the crayons on the bottom shelf to make them _____ to the young children.
a. accessible
b. receptive
c. eloquent
d. ambiguous

319. My computer was state-of-the-art when I bought it five years ago, but now it is _____.
a. current
b. dedicated
c. unnecessary
d. outmoded

320. Lola had been traveling for weeks; she was on a _____ to find the perfect cup of coffee.
a. surge
b. quest
c. discovery
d. cadence

321. Roland developed an _____ plan to earn extra money to buy the bell bottoms he had always wanted.
a. elitist
b. irrational
c. aloof
d. ingenious

322. George is _____ because he is the only one on staff who knows how to use this computer program.
a. frustrated
b. prudent
c. indispensable
d. creative

323. Harrison needs help; he's a _____ gambler.
a. cheerful
b. phantom
c. bucolic
d. chronic

324. I do not like your negative attitude, and it has _____ affected our working relationship.
a. favorably
b. adversely
c. shamelessly
d. candidly

SET 16 (Answers begin on page 130.)

Choose the word that best fills the blank in the following sentences.

325. It's easy to take care of my cousin's dog Sparky; he's a _____ and obedient pet.
   a. delectable
   b. commonplace
   c. meddlesome
   d. docile

326. I had no trouble finding your house; your directions were _____.
   a. priceless
   b. arduous
   c. explicit
   d. embodied

327. Though the principal had expected an uproar when he canceled the senior class trip, both parents and students seemed _____.
   a. enraged
   b. apathetic
   c. suspicious
   d. evasive

328. Make sure that drinking water is _____; otherwise, you could get sick.
   a. valid
   b. quenchable
   c. impure
   d. potable

329. I will vote in favor of the new city ordinance because it _____ many of the points we discussed earlier this year.
   a. encompasses
   b. releases
   c. reminisces
   d. disperses

330. Rachel _____ a plan to become a millionaire by age thirty.
   a. devised
   b. conformed
   c. decreased
   d. condoned

331. Joel ran away because he was _____ by the hedgehog.
   a. tolerated
   b. disillusioned
   c. consoled
   d. intimidated

332. Robert was in a _____ about which tie to buy.
   a. prestige
   b. redundancy
   c. quandary
   d. deficit

333. Jessica needs an A in her class, so studying for exams takes _____ over watching the Academy Awards.
   a. precedence
   b. conformity
   c. perplexity
   d. endeavor

334. Jane wanted to be _____, so she wore her bright yellow dress with the pink bows to the picnic.
a. eminent
b. virtuous
c. conspicuous
d. obscure

335. Whitney fell asleep during the movie because it had a(n) _____ plot.
a. monotonous
b. torrid
c. ample
d. vital

336. Barney _____ to go back to school to study dog grooming.
a. relied
b. surmised
c. presumed
d. resolved

337. Your drawing is a fair _____ of my family as the infamous Doppler gang.
a. portrayal
b. council
c. desolation
d. degeneration

338. When I let go of the handlebars, my bike _____ down the hill and splashed into a duck pond.
a. dissented
b. ventilated
c. careened
d. agitated

339. My sister decided to change her diet when the sour milk on her cereal gave off a _____ odor.
a. pungent
b. virtuous
c. fraudulent
d. frugal

340. The five o'clock whistle _____ announces the end of the workday at the largest toothpaste factory in town.
a. approvingly
b. significantly
c. symbolically
d. audibly

341. Jade was so hungry after her workout that she _____ gobbled up the caviar.
a. dynamically
b. voraciously
c. generously
d. beneficially

342. A small _____ occurred when my car door nicked the fender of a neighboring motor scooter.
a. mishap
b. attraction
c. reflex
d. duplicate

SET 17 (Answers begin on page 131.)

Choose the word that best fills the blank in the following sentences.

343. Columbus _____ believed that the world was round.
  a. optionally
  b. viciously
  c. prominently
  d. legitimately

344. Jeffrey was visibly nervous and spoke _____ about his upcoming appointment with his lawyer.
  a. warily
  b. luxuriously
  c. measurably
  d. narrowly

345. "I'm too young to date older men," Mandy said _____ when the high school senior asked her for a date.
  a. shapely
  b. coyly
  c. poorly
  d. totally

346. When Wayne found out that he had won the contest, he developed an _____ attitude, and we all had to listen to him crow about his accomplishments.
  a. arrogant
  b. achievable
  c. enlightened
  d. objective

347. Andrew showed _____ disregard for his pickup when he neglected to replenish the oil after the warning light came on.
  a. wanton
  b. admissive
  c. pretentious
  d. eloquent

348. Denise showed great _____ when she refused to discuss what was on the final exam in her economics class.
  a. substance
  b. generosity
  c. obligation
  d. integrity

349. The hail _____ the corn until the entire crop was lost.
  a. belittled
  b. pummeled
  c. rebuked
  d. commended

350. One of Angelo's _____ is collecting antique lemon juicers.
  a. eccentricities
  b. disappointments
  c. admonitions
  d. idioms

351. The motel offered a _____ after our long drive in the Grand Canyon.
  a. relapse
  b. respite
  c. brevity
  d. median

352. Margot brought large garbage bags to
_____ our cleanup along Route 66.
a. confound
b. pacify
c. integrate
d. facilitate

353. Her excellent bobsledding skills during the
competition _____ what we all hoped to
master.
a. prevailed
b. diverged
c. exemplified
d. varied

354. The _____ of sunshine and warm
weather made for a happy vacation at the
beach.
a. assumption
b. confluence
c. seclusion
d. treatise

355. Do you have the _____ papers to partici-
pate in the study on the effects of smoking?
a. punitive
b. grandiose
c. restorative
d. requisite

356. Don't _____ yourself: you must pass that
exam to graduate.
a. delude
b. depreciate
c. relinquish
d. prohibit

357. When you write your paper about *The Catcher
in the Rye*, please be sure to give a _____
description of the main character.
a. principled
b. determined
c. comprehensive
d. massive

358. Although Mary was _____ when we first
met her, she soon came to talk more than any
of us.
a. customary
b. reticent
c. animated
d. voluntary

359. Making money is a _____ to paying
taxes.
a. tedium
b. precursor
c. preference
d. momentum

360. Stacy _____ told the press that she
had accepted the nomination as board
chairperson.
a. repulsively
b. reputedly
c. perpetually
d. principally

SET 18 (Answers begin on page 132.)

Choose the word that best fills the blank in the following sentences.

361. After an hour of heavy rain, the storm _____ and we were able to get back out on the golf course.
  a. abated
  b. germinated
  c. constricted
  d. evoked

362. After years of experience, Wendy became the _____ veterinarian, performing surgery with ease.
  a. acute
  b. superficial
  c. consummate
  d. ample

363. Anthony tended the goldfish _____ when his neighbors were on vacation.
  a. terminally
  b. perpendicularly
  c. assiduously
  d. essentially

364. The kinds of lurid, violent movies being produced now are a sad _____ society's morals.
  a. generalization about
  b. analysis of
  c. review of
  d. commentary on

365. The little Tyler boys got in trouble for _____ fish out of Mr. Crumm's pond.
  a. riling
  b. poaching
  c. provoking
  d. smuggling

366. The two cats could be _____ only by the number of rings on their tails; otherwise, they were exactly alike.
  a. separated
  b. divided
  c. disconnected
  d. differentiated

367. The room was _____, the bed unmade and the dishes dirty; mice and cockroaches were everywhere.
  a. squalid
  b. squeamish
  c. queasy
  d. licentious

368. The drive was dangerous because of the rain; on each slick, wet curve I was afraid we would _____ into a ditch.
  a. operate
  b. hydroplane
  c. submerge
  d. reconnoiter

369. Madame Zirantha was an experienced fortune-teller and _____, so she knew everything about the occult.
  a. dreamer
  b. comedian
  c. criminal
  d. clairvoyant

370. Suddenly, the ghost in the corner of the room let out a(n) _____ shriek.
a. unearthly
b. covert
c. abstruse
d. esoteric

371. Our tiny boat spun into the _____, and we were sure that all hope was lost.
a. matrix
b. paradox
c. vector
d. vortex

372. The old man was _____; he refused to leave his home, even when told the volcano was about to erupt.
a. recitative
b. redundant
c. repatriated
d. recalcitrant

373. The project seemed _____, so we all applied ourselves to it with enthusiasm.
a. implacable
b. feasible
c. incorrigible
d. irreparable

374. The many colors in the swarm of butterflies seemed to create a(n) _____ cloud.
a. incandescent
b. iridescent
c. luminescent
d. cumulous

375. Mike and Jamal had perfect _____, each seeming to know, without being told, what the other felt.
a. stability
b. equilibrium
c. rapport
d. symmetry

376. In a(n) _____ voice, he told us all to sit down and shut up.
a. clamorous
b. flocculent
c. affable
d. strident

377. Now that she is a teenager, my daughter is _____ to talk about virtually all personal topics—she simply sits and stares at me.
a. synchronous
b. unanimous
c. indentured
d. reticent

378. The newspaper account of Cher's latest plastic surgery was completely erroneous, so she demanded a(n) _____.
a. abolition
b. invalidation
c. retraction
d. annulment

379. Because the smoking gun was found in the defendant's hand as he bent over the body, his guilt is _____.
a. incomparable
b. inimitable
c. incontrovertible
d. inconspicuous

SET 19 (Answers begin on page 133.)

Choose the word that best fills the blank in the following sentences. For each sentence you will have a pair of words to choose from. The pairs contain words that are easily confused and commonly misused.

380. Jane _____ first aid to the child with the broken arm.
   a. administered
   b. ministered

381. Enrique was _____ to see his kids after his long vacation.
   a. eager
   b. anxious

382. The judge set a huge amount for bail to _____ that the man would return to court.
   a. ensure
   b. insure

383. I turned green and became _____ after I rode the Super Loops ten times.
   a. nauseous
   b. nauseated

384. She looks fabulous in that dress; it fits _____.
   a. good
   b. well

385. The United States _____ 50 states.
   a. composes
   b. comprises

386. If I lose all of my savings gambling in Las Vegas, I will be profoundly _____.
   a. discomfited
   b. discomforted

387. All of the police officers were _____ witnesses because they actually saw the accident.
   a. credible
   b. credulous

388. His constant whistling _____ me like nothing else does.
   a. annoys
   b. aggravates

389. Dogs _____ to the cold weather when their fur grows thick.
   a. adapt
   b. adopt

390. A vitamin a day is part of a _____ diet.
   a. healthy
   b. healthful

391. If you see fit to _____ me into the hall of fame, I will pay you for it.
   a. deduct
   b. induct

392. This book is an _____ study of the Mayan culture.
   a. exhaustive
   b. exhausting

393. Because of her new baby it was not _____ for Mary to attend her high school reunion.
   a. feasible
   b. possible

394. The mail carrier _____ puts my neighbor's mail in my box.
   a. continuously
   b. continually

395. We will _____ with the plan we made earlier this month.
   a. proceed
   b. precede

396. Before buying a house you should seek the _____ of a qualified attorney.
   a. counsel
   b. council

397. In most classes homework is _____.
   a. compulsive
   b. compulsory

398. Her students appreciate Professor Diamond's _____ grading system.
   a. judicial
   b. judicious

399. Sam drove carefully on the _____ canyon road.
   a. tortuous
   b. torturous

SET 20 (Answers begin on page 134.)

For the following questions, choose the dictionary definition of the underlined word or phrase that best fits the sentence.

400. This incident will soon <u>blow</u> over.
   a. burn out or melt
   b. overwhelm
   c. be released or let out
   d. be forgotten

401. They <u>charge</u> $25 for a hamburger.
   a. set or ask a price of
   b. demand payment from
   c. blame or accuse
   d. hold financially liable for

402. On New Year's Eve, my friends and I went out on a merry <u>round</u> of parties that lasted until three A.M.
   a. complete course, succession, or series
   b. moving in a circle or about an axis
   c. one drink per person in a group
   d. interval of play in a game or sport

403. She is still with us in <u>spirit</u>.
   a. mind and emotions as distinguished from the physical body
   b. supernatural being, such as a ghost
   c. strong loyalty or dedication
   d. a mood or emotional state characterized by vigor or animation

404. The police decided that the accusation was the result of a simple <u>case</u> of mistaken identity.
   a. evidence offered in support of a claim
   b. legal action or suit
   c. peculiar or eccentric person
   d. instance or example

405. She <u>drew</u> me aside to tell me a secret.
   a. caused to move in a given direction
   b. caused to flow forth
   c. pulled so as to cover or uncover
   d. took or pulled out

406. Our soldiers did not stand a <u>ghost</u> of a chance against the enemy onslaught.
   a. returning memory or image
   b. spirit of a deceased person
   c. slight trace or bit
   d. faint, false photographic image

407. His conviction for fraud was a <u>gross</u> injustice.
   a. exclusive of deductions
   b. flagrant
   c. coarse
   d. corpulent

408. All night long we heard the waves <u>lap</u> against our lifeboat.
   a. to fold or wind around something
   b. to envelop in something or to swathe
   c. to wash against with a gentle slapping sound
   d. to place or lay a thing so as to cover part of another

409. Before I could <u>frame</u> an answer to his first question, he asked me another one.
a. formulate
b. rig evidence
c. enclose
d. physically construct

410. His request was refused because he did not go through the proper <u>channels</u>.
a. specified frequency bands
b. passages through which things can be moved or directed
c. official routes of communication
d. trenches, furrows, or grooves

411. We covered the antique dresser with a thin <u>coat</u> of varnish.
a. garment
b. pelt
c. integument
d. glaze

412. Bruno had to <u>gear</u> up for the big game.
a. prepare for action
b. adjust so as to fit or blend
c. a toothed wheel
d. equipment required for a particular activity

413. I threw my bowl of oatmeal and hit my sister <u>flush</u> in the face.
a. flow and spread out suddenly
b. evenly, in one plane
c. squarely or solidly
d. with margins aligned

414. The *SS Curmudgeon* began to <u>list</u> to one side, and we were afraid it would capsize.
a. choose
b. itemize
c. register
d. incline

415. Ed will <u>fly</u> into a rage when he learns you stole his socks.
a. rush, hasten
b. flee, escape
c. react explosively
d. rise in the air

SET 21 (Answers begin on page 134.)

For the following questions, choose the dictionary definition of the underlined word or phrase that best fits the sentence.

416. Ever since he fell off his tractor in 1947, my Uncle Pete has had a <u>game</u> leg.
 a. plucky
 b. score
 c. lame
 d. ready and willing

417. He had the <u>gall</u> to try to borrow my new car, after he had wrecked my old one.
 a. bitterness or rancor
 b. impudence or effrontery
 c. exasperation or vexation
 d. to damage or abrade

418. Clarissa and Calvin were a <u>match</u> made in heaven.
 a. a person or thing that is exactly like another
 b. an athletic contest or game
 c. two persons or things that harmonize with each other
 d. two objects fitted together

419. The landlord <u>doesn't mind</u> my having a cat, as long as I pay a $50 pet deposit.
 a. is not cautious or careful about
 b. is not aware of
 c. does not heed in order to obey
 d. is not concerned or troubled about

420. We had a <u>fan</u> to cool us off, but no place to plug it in.
 a. machine for winnowing
 b. wedge-shaped, paper, cooling device
 c. devotee
 d. device for circulating air

421. A <u>line</u> of oak trees borders the property.
 a. a length of material used for measuring
 b. an arrangement in an orderly series
 c. a chronological series
 d. something that is elongated and narrow

422. Congressman Axelrod shocked his constituents by deciding to <u>bolt</u> from his political party.
 a. gulp
 b. blurt out
 c. move or spring suddenly
 d. break away from

423. Buster's not very smart, but he's a good <u>egg</u>.
 a. fellow
 b. ovoid
 c. gamete
 d. bird product

424. When the police asked if she had been at the scene of the crime, she began to <u>hem</u> and haw.
 a. stitch down an edge of cloth
 b. equivocate
 c. enclose
 d. surround and shut in

425. *Home, home on the <u>range</u> / Where the deer and the antelope play . . .*
  a. area or sphere in which an activity takes place
  b. extensive area of open land
  c. place for shooting at targets
  d. stove with several burners

426. The President has finished appointing his <u>cabinet</u>.
  a. kind of wood, such as oak, walnut, or teak
  b. upright repository
  c. body of official advisors
  d. small, private room set apart for special activities

427. The contractor who built our house <u>pitched</u> the roof at a steep angle.
  a. plunge or fall forward
  b. set at a specified downward slant
  c. set in a particular key
  d. throw from a mound

428. Lefty was arrested when he tried to <u>fence</u> those TV sets.
  a. enclose within a structure
  b. sell pilfered goods
  c. fight with swords
  d. avoid giving a direct answer

429. The hydraulic <u>ram</u> malfunctioned, so work on the reservoir had to be stopped for the day.
  a. male sheep
  b. astrological sign
  c. projection on the prow of a ship
  d. water pump

430. Chet gave the first <u>draft</u> of his business report to his manager.
  a. a portion poured out or mixed
  b. the force required to move a load
  c. a preliminary sketch, outline, or version
  d. the act of selecting an individual without his consent

431. Wallace <u>represents</u> himself as the most honest attorney in town.
  a. to describe as having a specified quality
  b. to recall in memory
  c. to serve as a sign or symbol of
  d. to protest something

SET 22 (Answers begin on page 135.)

In each sentence, replace the italicized word or phrase with a more descriptive word or phrase that means the same thing.

432. Norbert's room is always *very clean*.
a. prim
b. pristine
c. stark
d. authentic

433. In the green meadow, we suddenly found our-selves surrounded by a *lot* of geese.
a. group
b. herd
c. bunch
d. gaggle

434. My friend Eleanor *really likes* hot, spicy food.
a. squanders
b. savors
c. lavishes
d. implores

435. The chairman of the board became angry, and the meeting ended *very quickly*.
a. abruptly
b. fitfully
c. ignominiously
d. discreetly

436. The letter was written in a heavy, ornate *hand-writing*.
a. words
b. copying
c. script
d. pennants

437. My room was at the end of *a grayish* hallway.
a. a disagreeable
b. an uninteresting
c. a bewitching
d. a dingy

438. He resisted the impulse to *pull* his hand away.
a. break
b. extract
c. yank
d. surmount

439. She watched the movements of his long, *clean* fingers.
a. lucid
b. immaculate
c. clear
d. extensive

440. I have *told my son not to eat* grease-laden, salty foods.
a. disabled my son not to eat
b. commissioned my son not to
c. prevented my son from eating
d. dissuaded my son from eating

441. In perfect time to the music, the little girls *moved in circles* across the stage.
a. rotated
b. shuffled
c. revolved
d. pirouetted

442. "What *a great party*!" the old gentleman shouted, as he downed his third martini.
a. an amusing gathering!
b. a fabulous wingding!
c. a timely assemblage!
d. a great ordering!

443. My bout with the flu has left me feeling <u>very weak</u>.
  a. debilitated
  b. capricious
  c. injurious
  d. forsaken

444. Displayed on the table was a *disordered group* of items.
  a. diverse aggregation
  b. variance
  c. hodgepodge
  d. denomination

445. A *row* of military vehicles moved slowly down the road.
  a. line
  b. satellite
  c. convoy
  d. column

446. Mom *walked* into the room and began rearranging things.
  a. harried
  b. spouted
  c. arose
  d. bustled

SET 23 (Answers begin on page 136.)

In each sentence, replace the italicized word or phrase with a more descriptive word or phrase that means the same thing.

447. All around them, daylight was *becoming* darkness.
   a. bedraggling into
   b. changing into
   c. eloping into
   d. slipping into

448. Georgina prevented a *disagreement* between Evan and Andrew.
   a. bramble
   b. squabble
   c. geyser
   d. perseverance

449. In the lamplight, his shadow *moved* along the wall.
   a. emigrated
   b. embellished
   c. lurched
   d. galvanized

450. Her short, gray hair was *set* in waves.
   a. glimmered
   b. guarded
   c. cloistered
   d. crimped

451. She proceeded with little *short* steps to the center of the room.
   a. mincing
   b. tiny
   c. miniature
   d. small

452. He *ate and drank* all the food on the table.
   a. divulged
   b. conversed
   c. consumed
   d. retracted

453. The *fruit dish* he ate for dessert actually left his stomach upset.
   a. nutriment
   b. peach cobbler
   c. apple carafe
   d. ripe platter

454. Rosanna put *blinking* lights in all her windows.
   a. scintillating
   b. satiny
   c. irradiated
   d. burnished

455. A *pile* of furniture blocked the entrance hall.
   a. flock
   b. bunch
   c. multitude
   d. jumble

456. The tall, old-fashioned chiffonier had long ago been *put in* the attic storage room.
   a. lapsed to
   b. banished to
   c. punctuated in
   d. sent to

457. A mysterious brown envelope *extended from* the mailbox.
   a. projected from
   b. languished from
   c. was seen in
   d. jutted out of

458. The women were adorned with necklaces and bracelets of *semi-precious stones*.
   a. some kind of jewels
   b. jewelry
   c. amethyst, topaz, and lapis-lazuli
   d. medium-priced mineral matter

459. She was *very happy* to greet her cousin, whom she hadn't seen in ten years.
   a. ecstatic
   b. edified
   c. efficacious
   d. egregious

460. Marvin's mood changed and he became *unfriendly* when I told him I wrecked his car.
   a. surly
   b. unsurpassed
   c. reckless
   d. vigilant

461. Depression descended on her like a *fog*.
   a. fable
   b. miasma
   c. countenance
   d. landscape

SET 24 (Answers begin on page 137.)

To answer the questions in this set, choose the word that comes closest to the meaning of the underlined word, or that fits best in the blank.

Answer questions 462–463 on the basis of the following passage.

Rhesus monkeys use facial expressions to communicate with each other and to enforce social order. For example, the "fear grimace," although it looks ferocious, is actually given by a _____ monkey who is intimidated by a _____ member of the group.

462. What is the meaning of the word "grimace" as it is used in the passage?
   a. smirk
   b. contortion
   c. howl
   d. simper

463. Which pair of words or phrases, if inserted into the blanks in sequence, makes the most sense in the writer's context?
   a. calm . . . aggressive
   b. dominant . . . subordinate
   c. confident . . . fearless
   d. subordinate . . . dominant

Answer questions 464–466 on the basis of the following passage.

John Reed was a schoolboy of fourteen years old; four years older than I, for I was but ten; large and _____ for his age, with a dingy and unwholesome skin; thick lineaments in a spacious visage, heavy limbs and large extremities. (From Charlotte Brönte's *Jane Eyre*)

464. Which word, if inserted in the blank, makes the most sense in the context of the passage?
   a. thin
   b. stout
   c. big
   d. pleasant

465. What is the meaning of the phrase "spacious visage" as it is used in the passage?
   a. large frame
   b. big face
   c. huge room
   d. dull expression

466. What is the meaning of the word "extremities" as it is used in the passage?
   a. hands and feet
   b. neck and shoulders
   c. arms and legs
   d. height and weight

Answer question 467 on the basis of the following passage.

Leo glared and looked _____ when he heard that his brother had won the oyster-eating contest.

467. Which word, if inserted in the blank, makes the most sense in the context of the passage?
   a. demure
   b. contrite
   c. askance
   d. analogous

Answer questions 468–470 on the basis of the following passage.

In this <u>refulgent</u> summer it has been a luxury to draw the breath of life. The grass grows, the buds burst, the meadow is spotted with fire and gold in the tint of flowers. The air is full of birds, and sweet with the breath of the pine, the <u>balm-of-Gilead</u>, and the new hay. Night brings no gloom to the heart with its welcome <u>shade</u>.
—*Ralph Waldo Emerson*

468. What is the meaning of the word "refulgent" as it is used in the passage?
   a. downhearted
   b. wholesome
   c. radiant
   d. stifling

469. To what does the phrase "balm-of-Gilead" most likely refer as it is used in the passage?
   a. a plant
   b. a cloud
   c. a meadow
   d. a scent

470. What is the meaning of the word "shade" as it is used in the passage?
   a. ghost
   b. obscurity
   c. darkness
   d. indistinctness

Answer questions 471–473 on the basis of the following passage.

In space flight there are the obvious _____ of meteors: debris and radiation; however, astronauts must also deal with two <u>vexing physiological foes</u>—muscle <u>atrophy</u> and bone loss.

471. Which word, if inserted in the blank, makes the most sense in the context of the passage?
   a. thrills
   b. ages
   c. hazards
   d. speed

472. The phrase "vexing physiological foes" as used in the paragraph refers to
   a. physical deterioration
   b. serious illness
   c. nervous disorder
   d. contagious disease

473. The word "atrophy" as used in the paragraph most nearly means
   a. pain
   b. wasting
   c. weakening
   d. cramping

Answer questions 474–476 on the basis of the following passage.

There are as many types of business correspondence as there are kinds of corporate <u>atmosphere</u>. As noted in Chapter 1, office environments range from small or medium traditional offices to little <u>quirky</u> entrepreneurial offices—some of them actually in garages, as Microsoft was years ago—to very formal, multinational <u>behemoths</u>.

474. What is the meaning of the word "atmosphere" as it is used in the passage?
   a. nerves
   b. ambiance
   c. vitality
   d. resources

475. What is the meaning of the phrase "quirky" as it is used in the passage?
   a. idiosyncratic
   b. cute
   c. quaint
   d. exceptional

476. Which of the following adjectives most likely describes a "behemoth"?
   a. enormous
   b. wealthy
   c. corrupt
   d. sinister

Answer questions 477–479 on the basis of the following passage.

The ravages [of the storm] were terrible in America, Europe, and Asia. Towns were <u>overthrown</u>, forests uprooted, coasts devastated by the mountains of water which were precipitated on them, vessels cast on the shore, whole districts <u>leveled</u> by waterspouts, several thousand people crushed on land or drowned at sea; such were the traces of its _____, left by this devastating tempest. —*Ralph Waldo Emerson*

477. What is the meaning of the word "overthrown" in the context of this passage?
a. invaded
b. devastated
c. raided
d. vanquished

478. What is the meaning of the word "leveled" as it is used in the passage?
a. completely destroyed
b. splashed
c. sprinkled
d. raised up

479. Which word, if inserted in the blank, makes the most sense in the context of the passage?
a. anger
b. fury
c. revenge
d. malevolence

Answer questions 480–481 on the basis of the following passage.

One summer, while visiting in the little village among the Green Mountains where her ancestors had dwelt for _____, my Aunt Georgiana kindled the <u>callow fancy</u> of my uncle, Howard Carpenter, then an idle, <u>shiftless</u> boy of twenty-one. —*Willa Cather*

480. Which word, if inserted in the blank, makes the most sense in the context of the passage?
a. days
b. a season
c. infinity
d. generations

481. What is the meaning of the word "shiftless" as used in the passage?
a. amiable
b. ruthless
c. lazy
d. easygoing

Answer questions 482–484 on the basis of the following passage.

A few species of bird are <u>parasitic</u>. The Glossy Cowbird, for example, lays five or six eggs a season, each in a different nest, and then abandons them. The Old World Cuckoo lays her <u>clutch</u> in the nest of the host that reared her, her young <u>ejecting</u> the host's offspring as soon as they are able.

482. In the context of the passage, to be "parasitic" is to
  a. take advantage of another without contributing anything
  b. devour a member of one's own species
  c. abandon one's offspring
  d. kill the offspring of another member of one's own species

483. As used in the passage, a clutch consists of
  a. eggs
  b. chicks
  c. feathers
  d. nests

484. What is the meaning of the word "ejecting" as used in the passage?
  a. fighting
  b. killing
  c. impinging on
  d. expelling

SET 25 (Answers begin on page 138.)

To answer the questions in this set, choose the word that comes closest to the meaning of the underlined word, or that fits best in the blank.

Answer questions 485–487 on the basis of the following passage.

Off-site disposal of regulated medical wastes remains a <u>viable option</u> for smaller hospitals (those with less than 150 beds). However, some <u>preliminary on-site processing</u>, such as <u>compaction</u>, may be necessary prior to sending the wastes off-site. Unfortunately, there is a serious problem with compaction. Although it reduces the total volume of solid wastes, often reducing transportation and disposal costs, it does not change the hazardous characteristics of the waste.

485. What is the meaning of the phrase "viable option" as it is used in the passage?
  a. good bet
  b. feasible choice
  c. serious concern
  d. definite decision

486. What is the meaning of the phrase "preliminary on-site processing" as it is used in the passage
  a. a reduction of waste bulk before taking it from hospital grounds
  b. disposal on hospital grounds of waste that can be broken down
  c. separating hazardous from non-hazardous waste
  d. loading of waste onto trucks in a safe and legally authorized manner

487. What is the meaning of the word "compaction" as it is used in the passage?
  a. consolidation
  b. grinding
  c. disintegration
  d. liquefying

Answer questions 488–489 on the basis of the following passage.

Martin Luther King was in Ghana when Ghana gained its independence. He said that the experience was an emotional one for him. As he watched the old flag, _____ British rule, lowered and the new flag of the <u>sovereign</u> nation raised, he wept.

488. Which word, if inserted into the blank, makes the most sense in the context of the passage?
  a. symbolizing
  b. regaling
  c. incorporating
  d. demanding

489. What is the meaning of the word "sovereign" as it is used in the passage?
  a. alone
  b. autonomous
  c. dominant
  d. commanding

Answer questions 490–492 on the basis of the following passage.

WARNING: Antihistamines can cause drowsiness, so you should avoid driving or other operations that demand alertness, coordination, or <u>dexterity</u>. Do not use this product if you are <u>intolerant to aspirin</u>. Allergic reactions may occur in <u>susceptible</u> persons.

490. What is the meaning of the word "dexterity" as it is used in the passage?
  a. balance
  b. manual skill
  c. manual strength
  d. gait

491. What is the meaning of the phrase "intolerant to aspirin" as it is used in the passage?
  a. unable to absorb aspirin without adverse effects
  b. dislike of the effects of aspirin
  c. unaffected by the healing effects of aspirin
  d. needing a stronger medication than aspirin

492. What is the meaning of the word "susceptible" as it is used in the passage?
  a. adaptable
  b. robust
  c. malleable
  d. sensitive

Answer questions 493–494 on the basis of the following passage.

The _____ use by physicians of medical abbreviations can cause medication errors and incorrect interpretation of notes in the medical chart. It can create treatment delay while the nurse seeks out the physician to ask for _____.

493. Which word, if inserted into the first blank, makes the most sense in the context of the passage?
  a. clandestine
  b. indiscriminate
  c. unlawful
  d. intrepid

494. Which word, if inserted into the second blank, makes the most sense in the context of the passage?
  a. reenactment
  b. restitution
  c. recompense
  d. clarification

Answer questions 495–497 on the basis of the following passage.

Adolescents are at risk of being both victims and perpetrators of violence. New violence-prevention programs in urban middle schools help reduce the crime rate by teaching both victims and perpetrators of such violence the skills of conflict resolution and how to apply reason to disputes, as well as by changing attitudes towards achieving respect through violence and towards the need to retaliate.

495. In the context of the passage, "perpetrators" are
   a. adolescents who are the victims of violence
   b. adolescents who commit violence
   c. community members who try to stop violence
   d. adult criminals who lure adolescents into violence

496. What is the meaning of the phrase "conflict resolution" as it is used in the passage?
   a. judging who is right and who is wrong
   b. asking for arbitration by an adult
   c. peaceful settlement of differences
   d. knowing when to call the authorities

497. What is the meaning of the word "retaliate" as it is used in the passage?
   a. settle for an unsatisfactory resolution to the problem
   b. determine who is stronger
   c. be consumed by hatred
   d. punish in kind or pay back

Answer questions 498–499 on the basis of the following passage.

The Wandering Albatross (*Diomedea exulans*) has a wing span of twelve feet and lays a single chalky egg in sand or in a simple grass nest. Sailors are said to catch Albatrosses with baited hooks let down into the ship's wake, then release them again, because to kill the Albatross is thought to be bad luck.

498. What is the most likely meaning of the word "chalky" as it is used in the passage?
   a. having the chemical makeup of chalk
   b. having the color of chalk
   c. tasting like chalk
   d. made of chalk

499. What is the meaning of the phrase "let down into the ship's wake" as it is used in the passage?
   a. lowered overboard alongside the ship
   b. tied to the railings that surround the ship's deck
   c. dangled into the turbulent water behind the ship
   d. dragged along the ship's deck

Answer questions 500–503 on the basis of the following passage.

Detectives who routinely investigate violent crimes can't help but become somewhat <u>jaded</u>. <u>Paradoxically</u>, the victims and witnesses with whom they work closely are often in a highly <u>vulnerable</u> and emotional state, usually feeling that they have been violated. Detectives must be trained to <u>handle</u> people in emotional distress and must be sensitive to the fact that for the victim the crime is not routine.

500. What is the meaning of the word "jaded" as it is used in the passage?
  a. angry at the people they serve and protect
  b. as street-wise as the criminals they have to deal with
  c. rendered insensitive by continued exposure to violent crime
  d. unconcerned about the safety of crime victims

501. Which of the following phrases makes most sense when substituted for the word "Paradoxically"?
  a. In contrast
  b. Similarly
  c. Unfortunately
  d. Deplorably

502. What is the meaning of the word "vulnerable" as it is used in the passage?
  a. frightened and unhappy
  b. defenseless and exposed
  c. numb and depressed
  d. suspicious and resentful

503. What is the meaning of the word "handle" as it is used in the passage?
  a. manage successfully
  b. control effectively
  c. manipulate efficiently
  d. deal with sympathetically

SET 26 (Answers begin on page 140.)

Each of the numbered blanks (504–523) in the passage below stands for a word that has been omitted. Read the whole passage to get an idea of what it is about, and then choose the word that best fits in each numbered blank.

Some people say there is too little respect for the law. I say there is **504)** _____ much respect for it. When people **505)** _____ the law too much, they will **506)** _____ it blindly. They will say, the majority has decided on this **507)** _____, therefore I must heed it. They will not **508)** _____ to consider whether or not the law is fair. If they do think the law is **509)** _____, they think it is even more wrong to **510)** _____ it. They **511)** _____ that people must not break the law but must live with it until the majority has been persuaded to **512)** _____ it. For example, many people in Birmingham, Alabama, knew that the laws that made black people **513)** _____ up their seats on buses to white people were **514)** _____. However, it was not **515)** _____ Rosa Parks (an otherwise law-abiding **516)** _____) refused to stand up and so **517)** _____ the law that change came about. I am not saying that we should **518)** _____ laws because they are **519)** _____ to us. I am saying that we must **520)** _____ to our consciences first. Only **521)** _____ should we follow the law. If we know in our **522)** _____ that the law is wrong, it is our **523)** _____ to break it.

504. a. very
b. too
c. over
d. not

505. a. respect
b. underestimate
c. obey
d. hinder

506. a. decide
b. believe
c. plan
d. follow

507. a. law
b. decision
c. candidate
d. minority

508. a. desire
b. think
c. stop
d. manage

509. a. righteous
b. wrong
c. tentative
d. just

510. a. discover
b. disobey
c. follow
d. respect

511. a. proclaim
b. believe
c. disagree
d. remark

512. a. disobey
b. make
c. change
d. observe

513. a. build
b. give
c. move
d. look

514. a. seemly
b. expeditious
c. untried
d. unjust

515. a. without
b. unless
c. for
d. until

516. a. citizen
b. authority
c. expatriot
d. felon

517. a. mocked
b. heeded
c. defied
d. justified

518. a. refuse
b. provide
c. break
d. deny

519. a. disastrous
b. inconvenient
c. proper
d. agreeable

520. a. listen
b. follow
c. obey
d. march

521. a. then
b. later
c. now
d. first

522. a. deliberations
b. fashion
c. hearts
d. feelings

523. a. mistake
b. duty
c. desire
d. choice

SET 27 (Answers begin on page 140.)

Each of the numbered blanks (524–543) in the passage below stands for a word that has been omitted. Read the whole passage to get an idea of what it is about, and then choose the word that best fits in each numbered blank.

Members of high-risk occupations like law enforcement and fire-fighting form tightly knit groups. The dangers they share naturally **524)** _____ them close, as does the knowledge that their **525)** _____ are sometimes in one another's hands. The bonds of loyalty and trust help police officers work more **526)** _____. However, the sense **527)** _____ loyalty can be taken to **528)** _____. Sometimes officers believe that they always must defend their comrades' actions. What happens though, **529)** _____ those actions are wrong? Frank Serpico found a disturbing **530)** _____ to that question. Serpico joined the New York City Police Department assuming that **531)** _____ moral standards were **532)** _____ of his fellow officers. When he found out otherwise, he was **533)** _____ with a dilemma: should he **534)** _____ the trust of his fellow officers by exposing the corruption, **535)** _____ should he close his **536)** _____ because loyalty to his fellow officers **537)** _____ all other moral (and legal) considerations? Serpico made his **538)** _____. Public attention was focused on police **539)** _____ and the NYPD was improved as a **540)** _____, but those improvements came at a tremendous personal **541)** _____ to Serpico. Ostracized and reviled by other officers, who felt **542)** _____, Serpico **543)** _____ left the force.

524.
a. bring
b. pry
c. locate
d. launch

525.
a. happiness
b. determination
c. situation
d. lives

526.
a. rapidly
b. effectively
c. sporadically
d. masterfully

527.
a. of
b. in
c. at
d. toward

528.
a. finality
b. fortune
c. extremes
d. power

529.
a. where
b. when
c. to
d. with

530.
a. difference
b. answer
c. danger
d. query

531. a. moderate
b. careful
c. unidentified
d. high

532. a. typical
b. sufferable
c. random
d. vital

533. a. encountered
b. motivated
c. faced
d. procured

534. a. garner
b. produce
c. enrage
d. violate

535. a. but
b. or
c. that
d. yet

536. a. investigation
b. intrigue
c. trial
d. arrangement

537. a. brought
b. beleaguered
c. outweighed
d. hindered

538. a. mark
b. payment
c. choice
d. fortune

539. a. camaraderie
b. corruption
c. apathy
d. support

540. a. measure
b. moment
c. predicament
d. result

541. a. reprimand
b. depreciation
c. debate
d. cost

542. a. betrayed
b. enlightened
c. confused
d. concerned

543. a. effortlessly
b. eventually
c. carefully
d. expertly

S·E·C·T·I·O·N 3

ANTONYMS

The following section consists of eight sets of antonyms, or words with opposite meanings. Many antonyms seem obvious (*good* and *bad, night* and *day, noisy* and *silent*), but others are not as easily recognizable. This is because many words have more than one meaning. For example, the word *clear* could mean *cloudless* or *transparent* or *unmistakable.* And, for each of those meanings *clear* has an opposite. If an antonym isn't obvious, think about other possible meanings of the word. Also, don't be fooled by answer choices that are synonyms. Remember that you are looking for a word that means the *opposite,* not a word that means the same.

SET 28 (Answers begin on page 141.)

544. Which word means the *opposite* of PROMPT?
  a. punctual
  b. slack
  c. tardy
  d. regular

545. What word is the *opposite* of DELAY?
  a. slow
  b. hasten
  c. pause
  d. desist

546. What word is the *opposite* of SOOTHE?
  a. increase
  b. comfort
  c. aggravate
  d. delight

547. Which word means the *opposite* of MODER-ATE?
  a. original
  b. average
  c. final
  d. excessive

548. Which word means the *opposite* of REVEAL?
  a. disclose
  b. achieve
  c. retreat
  d. conceal

549. Which word means the *opposite* of INITIAL?
  a. first
  b. crisis
  c. final
  d. right

550. Which word means the *opposite* of BRITTLE?
  a. flexible
  b. breakable
  c. grating
  d. thin

551. Which word means the *opposite* of CAPABLE?
  a. unskilled
  b. absurd
  c. apt
  d. able

552. What word is the *opposite* of STRAY?
  a. remain
  b. inhabit
  c. wander
  d. incline

553. What word is the *opposite* of DAINTY?
  a. delicate
  b. coarse
  c. harsh
  d. delicious

554. Which word means the *opposite* of CRAVING?
  a. desire
  b. repudiation
  c. motive
  d. repugnance

555. Which word means the *opposite* of FEROCIOUS?
  a. docile
  b. savage
  c. explosive
  d. noble

556. Which word means the *opposite* of GRUELING?

    a. effortless

    b. casual

    c. exhausting

    d. empty

557. Which word means the *opposite* of FORSAKE?

    a. admit

    b. abandon

    c. submit

    d. cherish

558. What word is the *opposite* of RESTRAIN?

    a. control

    b. liberate

    c. maintain

    d. distract

559. What word is the *opposite* of BLEAK?

    a. desperate

    b. dreary

    c. bright

    d. fond

SET 29 (Answers begin on page 141.)

560. What word is the *opposite* of UNRULY?
a. controllable
b. disorderly
c. honest
d. covered

561. What word is the *opposite* of ALERT?
a. attentive
b. inattentive
c. careful
d. trivial

562. Which word means the *opposite* of SOLIDARITY?
a. union
b. disunity
c. laxity
d. rigidity

563. Which word means the *opposite* of RETRACT?
a. assert
b. withdraw
c. impugn
d. follow

564. Which word means the *opposite* of BRIEF?
a. generous
b. lengthy
c. loose
d. concise

565. Which word means the *opposite* of OMIT?
a. eliminate
b. perform
c. depart
d. include

566. Which word means the *opposite* of CAUTIOUS?
a. considerate
b. noble
c. proper
d. reckless

567. Which word means the *opposite* of PROHIBIT?
a. surrender
b. permit
c. involve
d. embrace

568. Which word means the *opposite* of DISCLOSE?
a. succeed
b. conceal
c. restrain
d. possess

569. Which word means the *opposite* of SHAMEFUL?
a. honorable
b. animated
c. fickle
d. modest

570. Which word means the *opposite* of VAGUE?
a. hazy
b. skilled
c. definite
d. tender

571. Which word means the *opposite* of STIFLE?
   a. encourage
   b. familiarize
   c. deny
   d. overcome

572. Which word means the *opposite* of BELITTLE?
   a. arrange
   b. compliment
   c. criticize
   d. presume

573. Which word means the *opposite* of AIMLESS?
   a. inactive
   b. faithful
   c. purposeful
   d. impartial

574. Which word means the *opposite* of VULNERABLE?
   a. frantic
   b. feeble
   c. strong
   d. complicated

575. Which word means the *opposite* of DISTRESS?
   a. comfort
   b. reward
   c. trouble
   d. compromise

SET 30 (Answers begin on page 142.)

576. Which word means the *opposite* of UNITY?
   a. discord
   b. stimulation
   c. consent
   d. neglect

577. Which word means the *opposite* of DETEST?
   a. prohibit
   b. hate
   c. examine
   d. admire

578. Which word means the *opposite* of VALIANT?
   a. instinctive
   b. cowardly
   c. cynical
   d. worthy

579. Which word means the *opposite* of LENIENT?
   a. capable
   b. impractical
   c. merciful
   d. domineering

580. Which word means the *opposite* of TARNISH?
   a. absorb
   b. endure
   c. shine
   d. sully

581. Which word means the *opposite* of
   MANDATORY?
   a. apparent
   b. equal
   c. optional
   d. required

582. Which word means the *opposite* of
   CHAGRIN?
   a. conviction
   b. irritation
   c. pleasure
   d. humanity

583. Which word means the *opposite* of
   COMMENCE?
   a. initiate
   b. adapt
   c. harass
   d. terminate

584. Which word means the *opposite* of
   CONSCIENTIOUS?
   a. careless
   b. apologetic
   c. diligent
   d. boisterous

585. Which word means the *opposite* of
   DEFICIENT?
   a. necessary
   b. complete
   c. flawed
   d. simple

586. Which word means the *opposite* of CLARIFY?
   a. explain
   b. dismay
   c. obscure
   d. provide

587. Which word means the *opposite* of GRANT?
   a. deny
   b. consume
   c. allocate
   d. provoke

588. Which word means the *opposite* of LUCID?
   a. ordinary
   b. turbulent
   c. implausible
   d. unclear

589. Which word means the *opposite* of IMPARTIAL?
   a. complete
   b. prejudiced
   c. unbiased
   d. erudite

590. Which word means the *opposite* of JUDICIOUS?
   a. partial
   b. litigious
   c. imprudent
   d. unrestrained

591. Which word means the *opposite* of DISSONANCE?
   a. harmony
   b. carefulness
   c. specificity
   d. value

592. Which word means the *opposite* of ERUDITE?
   a. uneducated
   b. polite
   c. unknown
   d. agitated

SET 31 (Answers begin on page 143.)

Choose the word that means the OPPOSITE or most nearly the opposite of the word in capitals.

593. REQUIREMENT
    a. plan
    b. consequence
    c. option
    d. accident

594. IRRITATE
    a. soothe
    b. drain
    c. resist
    d. solve

595. PUNCTUAL
    a. random
    b. smooth
    c. intermittent
    d. tardy

596. VIRTUE
    a. reality
    b. fact
    c. vice
    d. amateur

597. HARMONY
    a. noise
    b. brevity
    c. safety
    d. discord

598. INSULT
    a. compliment
    b. contempt
    c. argument
    d. attitude

599. GENERAL
    a. specific
    b. total
    c. insignificant
    d. substantial

600. FORTUNATE
    a. excluded
    b. hapless
    c. hardworking
    d. lucky

601. IMAGINARY
    a. sober
    b. ordinary
    c. unrealistic
    d. factual

602. DEMOLISH
    a. attend
    b. consider
    c. create
    d. stifle

603. NOTABLE
    a. oral
    b. graceful
    c. legal
    d. ordinary

604. PRIM
- a. outrageous
- b. last
- c. ugly
- d. cantankerous

605. PROSPEROUS
- a. affluent
- b. destitute
- c. cowardly
- d. receptive

606. ABSORB
- a. acquire
- b. repel
- c. consume
- d. assist

607. CRITICAL
- a. inimical
- b. judgmental
- c. massive
- d. trivial

608. NIMBLE
- a. sturdy
- b. sluggish
- c. thoughtless
- d. relaxed

609. TRANQUIL
- a. agitated
- b. explicit
- c. sluggish
- d. composed

610. SPRIGHTLY
- a. eagerly
- b. loftily
- c. dully
- d. locally

611. INFANTILE
- a. despicable
- b. adolescent
- c. mature
- d. perpetual

612. IMPULSIVE
- a. secure
- b. mandatory
- c. rash
- d. cautious

613. AMIABLE
- a. dangerous
- b. permissive
- c. aloof
- d. congenial

614. COMPETENT
- a. incomplete
- b. intense
- c. incapable
- d. massive

615. PROMOTE
- a. explicate
- b. curtail
- c. concede
- d. retain

SET 32 (Answers begin on page 144.)

Choose the word that means the OPPOSITE or most nearly the opposite of the word in capitals.

616. PRUDENT
   a. rash
   b. licentious
   c. libertine
   d. demonstrative

617. RETAIN
   a. withhold
   b. release
   c. succumb
   d. incise

618. SCANT
   a. pellucid
   b. meager
   c. copious
   d. vocal

619. STEADFAST
   a. envious
   b. fickle
   c. improvident
   d. sluggish

620. STRINGENT
   a. obese
   b. lax
   c. obtuse
   d. fluid

621. SUBJECTIVE
   a. invective
   b. objectionable
   c. unbiased
   d. obedient

622. SUCCINCT
   a. distinct
   b. laconic
   c. unpersuasive
   d. verbose

623. TEDIOUS
   a. stimulating
   b. alarming
   c. intemperate
   d. tranquil

624. UNIFORM
   a. dissembling
   b. diverse
   c. bizarre
   d. slovenly

625. WARY
   a. alert
   b. leery
   c. worried
   d. careless

626. NOVEL
   a. dangerous
   b. unsettled
   c. suitable
   d. old

627. FALLACY
   a. truth
   b. blessing
   c. weakness
   d. fable

628. EXONERATE
   a. minimize
   b. respect
   c. irritate
   d. blame

629. SUBSEQUENT
   a. necessary
   b. insignificant
   c. primary
   d. previous

630. NONCHALANT
   a. intelligent
   b. popular
   c. concerned
   d. reckless

631. EXCISE
   a. sleep
   b. retain
   c. organize
   d. staple

632. DISPERSE
   a. gather
   b. agree
   c. praise
   d. satisfy

633. PREVARICATION
   a. ignorance
   b. veracity
   c. courtesy
   d. serenity

634. MIRTH
   a. height
   b. solemnity
   c. expense
   d. preparation

635. LIBERATE
   a. conserve
   b. restrain
   c. attack
   d. ruin

636. FALTERING
   a. steady
   b. adoring
   c. explanatory
   d. reluctant

637. OPTIMUM
   a. mediocre
   b. victorious
   c. worst
   d. rational

638. EPHEMERAL
   a. internal
   b. enduring
   c. temporary
   d. hidden

SET 33 (Answers begin on page 145.)

Choose the word that means the OPPOSITE or most nearly the opposite of the word in capitals.

639. ORIENT
  a. confuse
  b. arouse
  c. deter
  d. simplify

640. LEVITATE
  a. plod
  b. undulate
  c. whisper
  d. sink

641. PACIFY
  a. complicate
  b. dismiss
  c. excite
  d. atomize

642. PLAUSIBLE
  a. insufficient
  b. apologetic
  c. unbelievable
  d. credible

643. AVIDLY
  a. partially
  b. unenthusiastically
  c. equally
  d. unkindly

644. MEEKLY
  a. mildly
  b. painfully
  c. forcefully
  d. politely

645. COMPLACENT
  a. concerned
  b. pleasant
  c. happy
  d. convinced

646. AMBIGUOUS
  a. apathetic
  b. certain
  c. equivocal
  d. indefinite

647. ESTEEM
  a. disrespect
  b. disregard
  c. dissent
  d. disabuse

648. ELOQUENT
  a. shabby
  b. fluent
  c. inarticulate
  d. plain

649. DETERRENT
  a. encouragement
  b. obstacle
  c. proponent
  d. discomfort

650. IMPERTINENT
   a. animated
   b. rude
   c. relentless
   d. polite

651. LUDICROUS
   a. absurd
   b. somber
   c. reasonable
   d. charitable

652. ARCHAIC
   a. tangible
   b. modern
   c. ancient
   d. haunted

653. SULLEN
   a. morose
   b. impetuous
   c. provocative
   d. jovial

654. AWE
   a. contempt
   b. reverence
   c. valor
   d. distortion

655. TAUT
   a. neutral
   b. relaxed
   c. rigid
   d. vague

656. RILE
   a. appease
   b. prosper
   c. oppress
   d. irk

657. MAR
   a. delineate
   b. bolster
   c. clarify
   d. repair

658. SKEPTIC
   a. innovator
   b. friend
   c. politician
   d. believer

659. PREDECESSOR
   a. successor
   b. antecedent
   c. descendant
   d. ancestor

660. HYPOTHETICAL
   a. uncritical
   b. actual
   c. specific
   d. imaginary

661. ENHANCE
   a. diminish
   b. improve
   c. digress
   d. deprive

SET 34 (Answers begin on page 146.)

Choose the word that means the OPPOSITE or most nearly the opposite of the word in capitals.

662. INTREPID
   a. belligerent
   b. consistent
   c. chivalrous
   d. fearful

663. METHODICAL
   a. erratic
   b. deliberate
   c. hostile
   d. deformed

664. LATENT
   a. slow
   b. tardy
   c. dormant
   d. active

665. AFFABLE
   a. disagreeable
   b. hollow
   c. simple
   d. eager

666. TREPIDATION
   a. distribution
   b. agitation
   c. fearlessness
   d. uniformity

667. AUSPICIOUS
   a. unpromising
   b. repulsive
   c. jealous
   d. inattentive

668. MILITANT
   a. expeditious
   b. judicious
   c. pacifistic
   d. creative

669. FURTIVELY
   a. silently
   b. openly
   c. mildly
   d. quickly

670. ENTICE
   a. excite
   b. tempt
   c. express
   d. repel

671. INGENUOUS
   a. useful
   b. infinite
   c. calculating
   d. immature

672. OSTENTATIOUS
   a. hilarious
   b. humble
   c. careful
   d. obnoxious

673. ENDORSE
   a. condemn
   b. recommend
   c. announce
   d. adopt

674. ACCEDE
   a. excel
   b. retard
   c. disapprove
   d. increase

675. COPIOUS
   a. redundant
   b. meager
   c. ample
   d. shy

676. AMBIVALENCE
   a. compensation
   b. decisiveness
   c. enthusiasm
   d. devotion

677. DIVERGENT
   a. persuasive
   b. identical
   c. incomplete
   d. malicious

678. PENSIVE
   a. nervous
   b. prejudiced
   c. dizzy
   d. thoughtless

679. DISCERNIBLE
   a. invisible
   b. recognizable
   c. paradoxical
   d. scornful

680. VACILLATE
   a. struggle
   b. bleed
   c. resolve
   d. liberate

681. ABHOR
   a. scare
   b. surprise
   c. desire
   d. inspire

682. CHORTLE
   a. rhyme
   b. moan
   c. gravel
   d. guess

683. RAUCOUS
   a. ambitious
   b. continuous
   c. significant
   d. calm

684. DEPLETE
   a. report
   b. conform
   c. replace
   d. revise

685. EQUANIMITY
   a. excellence
   b. judgment
   c. compatibility
   d. perplexity

SET 35 (Answers begin on page 147.)

Choose the word that completes the analogy.

686. *Scarcely* is to *mostly* as *quietly* is to
a. secretly
b. rudely
c. loudly
d. silently

687. *Candid* is to *indirect* as *honest* is to
a. frank
b. wicked
c. truthful
d. devious

688. *Meaningful* is to *insignificant* as *essential* is to
a. unnecessary
b. important
c. unremarkable
d. basic

689. *Simple* is to *complex* as *trivial* is to
a. inconspicuous
b. significant
c. permanent
d. irrelevant

690. *Elated* is to *despondent* as *enlightened* is to
a. aware
b. ignorant
c. miserable
d. tolerant

691. *Divulge* is to *conceal* as *conform* is to
a. differ
b. construe
c. retain
d. offer

692. *Admire* is to *despise* as *praise* is to
a. ravage
b. surrender
c. admonish
d. warn

693. *Advance* is to *retreat* as *curtail* is to
a. damage
b. discard
c. consume
d. prolong

694. *Gratuitous* is to *expensive* as *sedentary* is to
a. active
b. legitimate
c. stable
d. selective

695. *Gluttonous* is to *abstemious* as *complimentary* is to
a. prominent
b. permissive
c. disparaging
d. calculating

696. *Trust* is to *suspicion* as *apex* is to
a. aperture
b. nadir
c. method
d. saga

697. *Deprivation* is to *affluence* as *capitulation* is to
a. resistance
b. potency
c. indigence
d. complacency

698. *Companion* is to *enemy* as *anonymity* is to
a. restraint
b. wealth
c. fame
d. anxiety

699. *Inebriated* is to *sober* as *atrocious* is to
a. pallid
b. haggard
c. sharp
d. noble

700. *Ornately* is to *plainly* as *blithely* is to
a. generously
b. morosely
c. cautiously
d. fervently

S·E·C·T·I·O·N 4

SPELLING

In this final section, you will practice your spelling skills with 301 different spelling questions. Many of the items involve commonly misspelled words, and the words range from easy to difficult. Some items ask you to choose the correctly spelled word; others ask you to choose the word that is misspelled. In Sets 46 and 47, you will find commonly confused homophones, words that sound alike but have different spellings and meanings. In the final four sets, you will be looking for misspelled words in sentences.

SET 36 (Answers begin on page 148.)

In each of the following sentences, choose the correct spelling of the missing word.

701. It is my _____ that the forest rangers in this state do a fine job.
a. beleif
b. bilief
c. belief
d. beleaf

702. She seems to have no _____ into her shoplifting problem.
a. insite
b. incite
c. ensight
d. insight

703. Richard is too _____ for his own good.
a. sinsitive
b. sensitive
c. sensative
d. sinsative

704. My sister is going to be on the cover of *Seventeen* _____.
a. magizine
b. magazene
c. magezine
d. magazine

705. Mysterious Marvin performs in _____ shows all around the country.
a. magic
b. magick
c. majic
d. maggic

706. The Healthy Living Vitamins Corporation is soon to be _____ for fraud.
a. prosecuted
b. prossecuted
c. prosecutted
d. proseccuted

707. Martin's outfit was quite _____ among all the gray suits.
a. conspiccuous
b. connspicuous
c. conspicuous
d. conspicious

708. The broccoli you bought will _____ up unless you put it in the refrigerator.
a. shrivel
b. shrivvel
c. shrivell
d. shrival

709. I just don't know what I'd do in her _____.
a. sittuation
b. situation
c. situachun
d. sitiation

710. Our basement apartment is so damp that my skin constantly feels _____.
a. clamby
b. clamy
c. clammy
d. clammby

711. It was a _____ day for the annual picnic.
a. superb
b. supperb
c. supurb
d. sepurb

712. The first time Wendy drove her new car into town, all her old friends were _____.
a. jellous
b. jealous
c. jealuse
d. jeolous

713. When we were halfway up the hill, we heard a _____ noise.
a. teriffic
b. terrific
c. terriffic
d. terific

714. If elected, my brother Roy will make a fine _____.
a. sherrif
b. sherriff
c. sherif
d. sheriff

715. Learning the words to all of Robert Frost's poetry has become an _____ for Jonathan.
a. obssession
b. obsessian
c. obsession
d. obsessiun

SET 37 (Answers begin on page 148.)

716. Officer Alvarez would have fired her weapon, but she did not want to place the hostage in
_____.

 a. jeoperdy
 b. jepardy
 c. jeapardy
 d. jeopardy

717. Because she was driving, Nora was unable to enjoy the _____ scenery.

 a. magniffisent
 b. magnifisent
 c. magnificent
 d. magnifficent

718. From inside the box came a strange
_____ whirring sound.

 a. mechinical
 b. mechanical
 c. mechenical
 d. machanical

719. The community was shocked when Cindy Pierce was arrested for selling _____ drugs.

 a. elicitt
 b. ellicit
 c. illicet
 d. illicit

720. There will be an immediate _____ into the cause of the accident.

 a. inquiry
 b. inquirry
 c. enquirry
 d. enquery

721. Al Guggins was taken to court after he attempted to _____ his contract with the city.

 a. terminate
 b. termenate
 c. terrminate
 d. termanate

722. Ben Alshieka feels that he is being
_____ for his beliefs.

 a. persecuted
 b. pursecuted
 c. presecuted
 d. perrsecuted

723. What on earth is that _____ odor?

 a. peculior
 b. peculiar
 c. peculliar
 d. puculior

724. Some people say that _____ is not a true science.

 a. psycology
 b. pyschology
 c. psychollogy
 d. psychology

725. Ronald Pinkington was twenty-seven years old before he got his driver's _____.

 a. lisense
 b. lisence
 c. lycence
 d. license

726. For Ed, the urge to eat chocolate proved to be
_____.
a. irresistible
b. irrisistible
c. iresistable
d. irresistable

727. In many states, road tests require
_____ parking.
a. paralel
b. paralell
c. parallal
d. parallel

728. The paramedics attempted to _____
the victim.
a. stabilize
b. stablize
c. stableize
d. stableise

729. Prosecutors argued that testimony concerning
the past behavior of the accused was
_____.
a. irelevent
b. irelevant
c. irrelevant
d. irrelevent

730. The mayor pointed to the _____
statistics.
a. encouredging
b. encouraging
c. incurraging
d. incouraging

SET 38 (Answers begin on page 149.)

731. Ophelia made a _____ to finish the work by Friday.
   a. commitment
   b. committment
   c. comittment
   d. comitment

732. Marcia's alibi seemed _____ on the face of it.
   a. rediculous
   b. rediculus
   c. ridiculous
   d. ridiculus

733. The large donation came from an _____ source.
   a. anynonimous
   b. anonimous
   c. anounymous
   d. anonymous

734. The scientists had to do an _____ amount of research.
   a. extraordinary
   b. extraordinery
   c. extrordinary
   d. ecstraordinary

735. The assistant manager gave his _____ that the report would be completed on time.
   a. asurrance
   b. assurance
   c. assurence
   d. assureance

736. The purpose of the new city ordinance was debated _____.
   a. frequently
   b. frequintly
   c. frequentlly
   d. frequentley

737. The _____ was placed on scientific evidence.
   a. enphasis
   b. emphisis
   c. emphasis
   d. emfasis

738. When paramedics arrived, the victim was in a _____ state.
   a. delirious
   b. dilerious
   c. delireous
   d. delirous

739. Each of the new employees had the same _____.
   a. asspiration
   b. asparation
   c. aspirration
   d. aspiration

740. The young man wished to _____ his right to speak freely.
   a. excercise
   b. exercise
   c. exersize
   d. exercize

741. The singer and her husband were a
_____ pair.
a. compattibl
b. compatable
c. compatible
d. commpatible

742. Theo is not _____ to eating this
much for dinner.
a. accustomed
b. accustommed
c. acustommed
d. acustomed

743. Sarah Renaldo will give the _____
address.
a. comencement
b. commencement
c. commencmment
d. comencmment

744. Who is your immediate _____?
a. superviser
b. supervizer
c. supervizor
d. supervisor

745. There are two types of _____: viral
and bacterial.
a. neumonia
b. pneumonia
c. pnumonia
d. newmonia

SET 39 (Answers begin on page 149.)

Write the plural of each of the following words.

746. piano   _____

747. sky   _____

748. mouse   _____

749. bunch   _____

750. strawberry   _____

751. shelf   _____

752. box   _____

753. deer   _____

754. stimulus   _____

755. son-in-law   _____

756. gas   _____

757. industry   _____

758. handful   _____

759. tomato   _____

760. crisis   _____

761. memorandum   _____

762. species   _____

763. antenna   _____

SET 40 (Answers begin on page 150.)

Complete the following words with either _ei_ or _ie_.

764. rec___ve

765. p___ce

766. r___gn

767. ___ther

768. w___ght

769. dec___ve

770. y___ld

771. caff___ne

772. fr___ndly

773. gr___f

774. effic___nt

775. conc___ted

776. ach___ve

777. for___gn

778. var___ty

779. pat___nt

780. qu___tly

SET 41 (Answers begin on page 150.)

For each of the following questions, find the word that is NOT spelled correctly. If all the words are spelled correctly, choose answer **d**.

781. a. women
   b. people
   c. babys
   d. no mistakes

782. a. radios
   b. leaves
   c. alumni
   d. no mistakes

783. a. anouncement
   b. advisement
   c. description
   d. no mistakes

784. a. omission
   b. aisle
   c. litrature
   d. no mistakes

785. a. informal
   b. servent
   c. comfortable
   d. no mistakes

786. a. vegetable
   b. width
   c. variation
   d. no mistakes

787. a. twentieth
   b. fortieth
   c. ninetieth
   d. no mistakes

788. a. association
   b. unecessary
   c. illegal
   d. no mistakes

789. a. villin
   b. volunteer
   c. voracious
   d. no mistakes

790. a. hindrence
   b. equipped
   c. possessive
   d. no mistakes

791. a. procedure
   b. judgment
   c. testamony
   d. no mistakes

792. a. explicit
   b. abduct
   c. rotate
   d. no mistakes

793. a. through
   b. threw
   c. thorough
   d. no mistakes

794. a. quantaty
b. quality
c. quaint
d. no mistakes

795. a. requirement
b. reverence
c. resistent
d. no mistakes

796. a. incorporate
b. contridict
c. exhale
d. no mistakes

797. a. pertain
b. reversel
c. memorization
d. no mistakes

798. a. marshal
b. martial
c. marshmellow
d. no mistakes

799. a. optimum
b. palpable
c. plunder
d. no mistakes

800. a. ravinous
b. miraculous
c. wondrous
d. no mistakes

SET 42 (Answers begin on page 151.)

For each of the following questions, find the word that is NOT spelled correctly. If all the words are spelled correctly, choose answer **d**.

801.
a. phenomonal
b. emulate
c. misconception
d. no mistakes

802.
a. mischief
b. temperture
c. lovable
d. no mistakes

803.
a. stadium
b. competitor
c. atheletic
d. no mistakes

804.
a. dictionary
b. auditorium
c. biology
d. no mistakes

805.
a. geometry
b. perimeter
c. circumferance
d. no mistakes

806.
a. general
b. corporal
c. lieutenant
d. no mistakes

807.
a. poltry
b. rhubarb
c. marmalade
d. no mistakes

808.
a. transparent
b. strenthen
c. lightning
d. no mistakes

809.
a. primarily
b. finallity
c. specifically
d. no mistakes

810.
a. parliament
b. governor
c. congressional
d. no mistakes

811.
a. religous
b. insurance
c. military
d. no mistakes

812.
a. mortar
b. outweigh
c. pursue
d. no mistakes

813.
a. balcony
b. delenquent
c. emergency
d. no mistakes

814. a. gratitude
b. horrendous
c. forcast
d. no mistakes

815. a. ketchup
b. condiment
c. relish
d. no mistakes

816. a. rightious
b. strenuous
c. manageable
d. no mistakes

817. a. sincerly
b. faithfully
c. reliably
d. no mistakes

818. a. label
b. kindergarden
c. medal
d. no mistakes

819. a. bookkeeping
b. accounting
c. bankrupcy
d. no mistakes

820. a. bungalow
b. construction
c. architecture
d. no mistakes

SET 43 (Answers begin on page 151.)

For each of the following questions, find the word that is NOT spelled correctly. If all the words are spelled correctly, choose answer **d**.

821. a. crusade
b. political
c. campain
d. no mistakes

822. a. digestion
b. resperation
c. circulation
d. no mistakes

823. a. potatoe
b. artichoke
c. cucumber
d. no mistakes

824. a. parachute
b. rehearsel
c. together
d. no mistakes

825. a. intrigued
b. hypnotized
c. fasinated
d. no mistakes

826. a. distructive
b. decisive
c. distinguished
d. no mistakes

827. a. evaporate
b. vanish
c. disolve
d. no mistakes

828. a. illuminate
b. enlighten
c. clarify
d. no mistakes

829. a. abolish
b. forfit
c. negate
d. no mistakes

830. a. zoology
b. meterology
c. anthropology
d. no mistakes

831. a. ajournment
b. tournament
c. confinement
d. no mistakes

832. a. vague
b. vacancy
c. vengence
d. no mistakes

833. a. tuition
b. mediocre
c. tremendus
d. no mistakes

834.
  a. integrity
  b. ingenuity
  c. immortality
  d. no mistakes

835.
  a. conjunction
  b. preposition
  c. capitolization
  d. no mistakes

836.
  a. narled
  b. knobby
  c. blemished
  d. no mistakes

837.
  a. brackets
  b. parenthisis
  c. ellipsis
  d. no mistakes

838.
  a. visionary
  b. virtuoso
  c. vigor
  d. no mistakes

839.
  a. language
  b. philosophy
  c. sonet
  d. no mistakes

840.
  a. depo
  b. aisle
  c. knight
  d. no mistakes

SET 44 (Answers begin on page 152.)

For each of the following questions, find the word that is NOT spelled correctly. If all the words are spelled correctly, choose answer **d**.

841. a. perscribe
b. deviate
c. plausible
d. no mistakes

842. a. association
b. personel
c. solidarity
d. no mistakes

843. a. playwright
b. dramatic
c. actor
d. no mistakes

844. a. specialized
b. negotiate
c. scruteny
d. no mistakes

845. a. abundant
b. bounteous
c. luxurient
d. no mistakes

846. a. bacheler
b. lyrical
c. inheritance
d. no mistakes

847. a. initial
b. graditude
c. influential
d. no mistakes

848. a. loosely
b. emancipate
c. muzzled
d. no mistakes

849. a. columm
b. business
c. acquisition
d. no mistakes

850. a. border
b. bullitin
c. competitor
d. no mistakes

851. a. ambassador
b. dignitary
c. embasy
d. no mistakes

852. a. jockey
b. equestrian
c. maneuver
d. no mistakes

853. a. nevertheless
b. neutral
c. neurotic
d. no mistakes

854. a. problematic
b. questionaire
c. controversial
d. no mistakes

855. a. disciple
b. sublime
c. zeneth
d. no mistakes

856. a. pungeant
b. aromatic
c. spicy
d. no mistakes

857. a. restle
b. persevere
c. joust
d. no mistakes

858. a. hybrid
b. hypnosis
c. hygenic
d. no mistakes

859. a. carriage
b. carburator
c. chauffeur
d. no mistakes

860. a. digestible
b. corrugated
c. currency
d. no mistakes

SET 45 (Answers begin on page 152.)

For each of the following questions, find the word that is NOT spelled correctly. If all the words are spelled correctly, choose answer **d**.

861. a. judicious
b. ilegal
c. magistrate
d. no mistakes

862. a. colosal
b. magnanimous
c. extravagant
d. no mistakes

863. a. correspondent
b. corosive
c. coronation
d. no mistakes

864. a. typhoid
b. typewriter
c. tyrenny
d. no mistakes

865. a. corrupt
b. malcontent
c. reinstate
d. no mistakes

866. a. fateague
b. weariness
c. tedium
d. no mistakes

867. a. acrobat
b. somersault
c. gymnist
d. no mistakes

868. a. gullable
b. credulous
c. immature
d. no mistakes

869. a. unscrupulous
b. vacency
c. mediocre
d. no mistakes

870. a. odious
b. contemptable
c. heinous
d. no mistakes

871. a. tuition
b. transcendent
c. tranquel
d. no mistakes

872. a. whether
b. weather
c. climate
d. no mistakes

873. a. traiter
b. renegade
c. revolutionary
d. no mistakes

874. a. manicle
b. shackle
c. yoke
d. no mistakes

875. a. volume
b. volitile
c. voluntary
d. no mistakes

876. a. murmur
b. lucrative
c. millionaire
d. no mistakes

877. a. regrettable
b. recognizable
c. reasonable
d. no mistakes

878. a. gluttonous
b. zealous
c. omniverous
d. no mistakes

879. a. fanaticism
b. zelotry
c. dogmatic
d. no mistakes

880. a. resilience
b. reostat
c. rhubarb
d. no mistakes

SET 46 (Answers begin on page 153.)

In each of the following sentences, choose the correct spelling of the missing word. All of the choices are sound-alikes (homophones) of each other, so you must choose which word has the correct meaning.

881. My favorite _____ is peach pie with chocolate ice cream.
   a. desert
   b. dessert

882. Do you think I should run for a seat on the city _____?
   a. counsel
   b. council

883. I paid $100 for this table, which was a very _____ price.
   a. fair
   b. fare

884. This is the _____ of the new art museum.
   a. sight
   b. cite
   c. site

885. Drive _____ the park at 5:00 this evening.
   a. buy
   b. bye
   c. by

886. George is Mary's _____ husband.
   a. fourth
   b. forth

887. When Hugh slammed on the _____, his car slid into the ditch.
   a. breaks
   b. brakes

888. Jennifer _____ the group on a hike into the wilderness.
   a. lead
   b. led

889. Have dinner with us at the restaurant; we'll meet you _____.
   a. they're
   b. their
   c. there

890. May I have a _____ of cheese?
   a. piece
   b. peace

891. You don't have a _____ to disturb the other workers.
   a. write
   b. rite
   c. right

892. Every night I exercise in my living room on my _____ bicycle.
   a. stationery
   b. stationary

893. At the beach, we went digging for clams and _____.
   a. mussels
   b. muscles

894. We _____ the exit and had to turn
around.
a. past
b. passed

895. The French Revolution was known as the
"_____ of Terror."
a. Rain
b. Reign
c. Rein

896. I don't understand today's math _____.
a. lesson
b. lessen

897. How will they store all that nuclear
_____?
a. waste
b. waist

898. Three _____ and four sophomores will
represent our school.
a. freshman
b. freshmen

899. This problem is _____ complex.
a. two
b. to
c. too

900. My grandmother is an _____ historian.
a. imminent
b. immanent
c. eminent

SET 47 (Answers begin on page 154.)

Choose the sentence in which the underlined word is NOT spelled correctly. If there are no mistakes, choose answer **d**.

901. a. I will take a <u>course</u> in economics next semester.
    b. Follow the river's <u>coarse</u>.
    c. Sandpaper is always <u>coarse</u>.
    d. No mistakes.

902. a. Do you want to meet at nine or ten? The <u>latter</u> is better for me.
    b. Let's go shopping <u>later</u> this week.
    c. <u>Later</u>, he told us of his plans to build a new house.
    d. No mistakes.

903. a. We will <u>bored</u> the plane at 4:00.
    b. The <u>board</u> members will all attend.
    c. He used his drill and <u>bored</u> a hole in the wall.
    d. No mistakes.

904. a. Terrence accidentally <u>poured</u> the milk onto the table.
    b. There were large <u>pores</u> in the soil.
    c. Josie <u>pours</u> over the catalogs she receives in the mail.
    d. No mistakes.

905. a. Roger was very <u>vane</u>; he often stood in front of the mirror.
    b. We studied the <u>veins</u> in the leaves.
    c. We put a weather <u>vane</u> on the roof.
    d. No mistakes.

906. a. The sun <u>shone</u> brightly.
    b. The house was <u>shown</u> to the real estate agent.
    c. Why wasn't I <u>shown</u> how to operate this machine?
    d. No mistakes.

907. a. They will <u>raze</u> this old building, and in its place, build a new skyscraper.
    b. <u>Raise</u> your hand if you know the answer.
    c. Cal <u>raises</u> chickens for a living.
    d. No mistakes.

908. a. Scotty is learning how to write <u>capital</u> letters.
    b. We don't have enough <u>capitol</u> to buy a new building.
    c. What is the <u>capital</u> of North Dakota?
    d. No mistakes.

909. a. The <u>great</u> majority of the class will attend the pep rally.
    b. Be sure to clean the <u>grate</u> in the fireplace.
    c. That music <u>greats</u> on my nerves.
    d. No mistakes.

910. a. I prefer to eat <u>plain</u>, home-cooked meals.
    b. Some people say it's a boring landscape, but I love the <u>planes</u> of Iowa and Nebraska.
    c. We need to use a <u>plane</u> to make the top of the door level.
    d. No mistakes.

911. a. There are <u>holes</u> in your socks.
    b. I found a <u>whole</u> set of dishes at a garage sale.
    c. He ate the <u>hole</u> pie.
    d. No mistakes.

912. a. What is the <u>morale</u> of the story?
    b. Have you no <u>moral</u> standards?
    c. Employee <u>morale</u> was low.
    d. No mistakes.

SET 48 (Answers begin on page 154.)

Choose the sentence that contains a misspelled word. If there are no mistakes, choose answer **d**.

913. a. We were disatisfied with the results of the experiment.
  b. Our company has a bounteous supply of sticky notes.
  c. Quit squandering your money.
  d. No mistakes.

914. a. Sally plays five different musical instruments.
  b. Use your dictatorial powers to get results.
  c. What are you wearing to the masquerade party?
  d. No mistakes.

915. a. Have you packed the antidote for snake bites?
  b. The new pharmicy has twenty-eight aisles.
  c. Read all of the stories in the anthology.
  d. No mistakes.

916. a. Mack sliced his finger with the meat cleaver.
  b. You have been more than charitable.
  c. Which president is buried in this cemetary?
  d. No mistakes.

917. a. He has revealed his innermost secrets.
  b. The show was called "Truth or Consequences."
  c. You think he's funny, but I think he's vulgar.
  d. No mistakes.

918. a. Her conversation was filled with sarcasim.
  b. I would like to be as poised as Susanna is.
  c. You can learn self-confidence.
  d. No mistakes.

919. a. After all, he is a bureaucrat.
  b. This room has the fragrence of lilacs.
  c. I fractured my toe on the chair leg.
  d. No mistakes.

920. a. His inaugeration speech was too long.
  b. There are too many people in the laundromat.
  c. Yuki is a nonconformist.
  d. No mistakes.

921. a. Read the labels on all the food you buy.
  b. Your new dress is lovily.
  c. Did you see the lightning?
  d. No mistakes.

922. a. I want to make a parachute jump.
  b. Carlos is a physical therapist.
  c. This story has received too much publisity.
  d. No mistakes.

923. a. Her contribution was significant.
  b. Save all of your receipts.
  c. Lena has three roommates.
  d. No mistakes.

924. a. Mercury is a poisonous substance.
  b. Todd spent twenty years in the militery.
  c. You are so immature!
  d. No mistakes.

925. a. She did not even aknowledge my presence.
b. Do you think this is an attainable goal?
c. For the fiftieth time, the answer is no.
d. No mistakes.

926. a. There is a warrant out for his arrest.
b. Measure both the length and the width of the table.
c. How many witnesses do we have?
d. No mistakes.

927. a. Harry is a sulky, pouting grouch.
b. We have a fundimental difference of opinion.
c. Your behavior can only be described as impolite.
d. No mistakes.

928. a. This virus is making me feverish.
b. Coffee is a stimulant.
c. Stop that incessant whining!
d. No mistakes.

929. a. After Zack joined the Marines, we took a picture of him in his unaform.
b. The tenants' association will hold their meeting tonight.
c. This is the best value you'll find anywhere.
d. No mistakes.

930. a. I'm taking my neice and nephew to the amusement park.
b. They made their announcement in Sunday's newspaper.
c. That is one argument that is never resolved.
d. No mistakes.

931. a. What is your assessment?
b. How much paint do we need to finish the job?
c. Your assignment is to write a four-page report.
d. No mistakes.

932. a. The odor coming from your refrigerator makes me nauseous.
b. He thinks all war is imoral.
c. Patrick's brain is spongy from all that television he watches.
d. No mistakes.

933. a. I'm planning to cook two turkeys on Thanksgiving.
b. Why did you refuse to accept his offer?
c. The trafic at rush hour is unbelievable.
d. No mistakes.

934. a. The dancer was graceful and elegent.
b. Is that horse a thoroughbred?
c. He is annoying and meddlesome.
d. No mistakes.

SET 49 (Answers begin on page 155.)

Choose the sentence that contains a misspelled word. If there are no mistakes, choose answer **d**.

935. a. Avery's thriftyness is sometimes a problem.
b. Marlene is dignified and self-assured.
c. You have given me the best advice I've ever had.
d. No mistakes.

936. a. Jed took an administrative position with the state department.
b. Erin works for a federal agency, too.
c. How many honest politicians do you know?
d. No mistakes.

937. a. The doctor's illustrious career began almost fifty years ago.
b. Rita and Roseanne are poler opposites.
c. Sam took a poll to see how many people were opposed.
d. No mistakes.

938. a. Barbara is very ambitious and knows how to set goals.
b. Vince bears a striking resemblence to Abraham Lincoln.
c. Do not ruin your good reputation.
d. No mistakes.

939. a. A cup of herb tea will sooth my nerves.
b. I received lots of encouragement from my science teacher.
c. Alcohol acts as a depressant.
d. No mistakes.

940. a. The orchestra played my favorite symphony.
b. After registration, we will know if enrollment is up or down.
c. We paid homage to the soldiers who fought in Vietnam.
d. No mistakes.

941. a. Meet me at a quarter after six.
b. He quareled frequently with the other members of his family.
c. She buys only quality merchandise.
d. No mistakes.

942. a. Curt will probibly stay home tonight.
b. The coach praised the team for last night's game.
c. It was a relief to learn that Brett had arrived safely.
d. No mistakes.

943. a. The movie was immensely popular.
b. Joshua made a commitment to practice the piano each day.
c. We did not know the correct pronouncia-tion.
d. No mistakes.

944. a. The speaker presented an idea that was foreign to us.
b. Marcus spoke directly to the governor.
c. The boys and girls in the chorus gave a stunning performance.
d. No mistakes.

945. a. The winners received their prizes several days ago.
b. The principle met with the members of the student council.
c. How many passengers traveled by train?
d. No mistakes.

946. a. The scedule was posted on the bulletin board.
b. Patrick made a solemn promise to arrive on time.
c. I have an indoor thermometer hanging in my kitchen.
d. No mistakes.

947. a. When will you have time to knit another sweater?
b. The light fixture has become a permanent part of the room.
c. I have no knowlege of how the bicycle was damaged.
d. No mistakes.

948. a. Bobby thought the team did not play aggressively.
b. The mayor and the city manager were not in agreement.
c. The basement of the building seemed more like a dungeon.
d. No mistakes.

949. a. The scizzors were not sharp enough.
b. The intense heat scorched my houseplants.
c. The Milky Way is only one of many galaxies.
d. No mistakes.

950. a. We knew that Ellen was embarassed.
b. I am teaching my brother to read mathematical symbols.
c. Neither Joe nor Gary has done the research for his report.
d. No mistakes.

951. a. Which of the following countries is not a democracy?
b. Occasionally, our dog Skippy will dig under the fence.
c. This weather is terribly depressing.
d. No mistakes.

952. a. All employees will be eligible for three weeks of vacation.
b. The managment team promised to look into the situation.
c. We saw an enormous animal running toward us.
d. No mistakes.

953. a. The commissioner has assumed responsibility.
b. Kate likes to visit with her nieghbor.
c. This is not a commonly held viewpoint.
d. No mistakes.

954. a. Edith and her sister closely resemble one another.
b. Her handwriting was barely legible.
c. The butterflies wings are perfectly symetrical.
d. No mistakes.

955.
a. Our company sent forty representatives to the meeting.
b. When did you realize that the theory could not be proven?
c. We both filled out an application for employment.
d. No mistakes.

956.
a. All of the musicians were well trained.
b. Thank you for your assistance.
c. You are required to follow standard proceedures.
d. No mistakes.

SET 50 (Answers begin on page 155.)

Choose the sentence that contains a misspelled word. If there are no mistakes, choose answer **d**.

957. a. I knew she was bored because she wriggled in her seat.
  b. If you want to succeed, please report to work imediately.
  c. He was conscious of his surroundings.
  d. No mistakes.

958. a. My mother will soon celebrate her fortieth birthday.
  b. Autumn is my favorite time of year.
  c. My cousin is going skiing in Feburary.
  d. No mistakes.

959. a. William is the most sensable person I know.
  b. The festival is held at a different time each year.
  c. It is not customary for the members to arrive late.
  d. No mistakes.

960. a. As treasurer, Jenny has the financial responsibility.
  b. I've been assured that this illness is not contagious.
  c. My mother says our neighbor is eccentric, but I say she's wierd.
  d. No mistakes.

961. a. I admire Rachel's abilities as a scholar.
  b. The senators will vote on two critical issues.
  c. Please pick up my prescription at the pharmacy.
  d. No mistakes.

962. a. Her father is a captin in the navy.
  b. The weather here changes frequently.
  c. We adopted a new policy.
  d. No mistakes.

963. a. Rita is a freshman; her sister is a sophmore.
  b. My grandfather was a distinguished professor.
  c. This is the most efficient way.
  d. No mistakes.

964. a. Did you memorize the grammer rules?
  b. I'll phone you tomorrow.
  c. Benedict Arnold was a traitor.
  d. No mistakes.

965. a. Pick up the car on Wednesday.
  b. Let's go shopping on Thursday.
  c. My birthday is on Saturday.
  d. No mistakes.

966. a. Do not be deterred.
  b. Which is most economical?
  c. We made a unanimus decision.
  d. No mistakes.

967. a. The painters forgot to take their ladder.
  b. You're making an irrational decision.
  c. This movie has been overated.
  d. No mistakes.

968. a. They began their ascent up the mountain.
b. That chair is ancient.
c. There is an abundant supply of wheat this year.
d. No mistakes.

969. a. The secretery of state appeared on the Sunday talk shows.
b. Do you know what a promissory note is?
c. We are unable to ascertain the truth.
d. No mistakes.

970. a. I think it's a mechanical problem.
b. His credentials are impecable.
c. Don't bother me now.
d. No mistakes.

971. a. Harrison is a confirmed television addict.
b. I'm pleased to make your acquaintence.
c. Is that a maple or a sycamore tree?
d. No mistakes.

972. a. There are many ways to increase your vocabulary.
b. Read the fourth chapter by next week.
c. You have thousands of choices.
d. No mistakes.

973. a. I'm telling you this for your own welfare.
b. He is undecided about which job to accept.
c. Unfortunatly, we don't have this sweater in another color.
d. No mistakes.

974. a. Is this word mispelled?
b. Safety is my primary concern.
c. We all are individual and unique.
d. No mistakes.

975. a. I prefer to take the bus.
b. You must have a balanced life.
c. Irene will study medicine next year.
d. No mistakes.

976. a. I'm going to wear my velvit pants.
b. These sentences are too vague.
c. George wrapped the birthday present.
d. No mistakes.

977. a. This is a new development.
b. I am truely sorry.
c. Rhoda has a private office.
d. No mistakes.

978. a. Edwin made his announcement yesterday.
b. Don't swim in that scummy water.
c. I want to buy a portable dishwasher.
d. No mistakes.

SET 51 (Answers begin on page 156.)

Choose the sentence that contains a misspelled word. If there are no mistakes, choose answer **d**.

979. a. What a magnifisent view!
   b. Today we're giving impromptu speeches.
   c. That's a legitimate concern.
   d. No mistakes.

980. a. There will be elaborate preparations.
   b. Who is responsible for this mess?
   c. He distributed the pamplet yesterday.
   d. No mistakes.

981. a. Elyse made a significant contribution.
   b. Did you hear that owl screech?
   c. Look at the siloette of the moon.
   d. No mistakes.

982. a. They hoped to avert a tragedy.
   b. The quartett sang at my sister's wedding.
   c. Don't patronize me.
   d. No mistakes.

983. a. I think we'll use lacquer to finish the table.
   b. The laboratory is down that hallway.
   c. Our friendship was irrepairably damaged.
   d. No mistakes.

984. a. There have been twenty burgleries in the neighborhood this year.
   b. He is the most belligerent person I have ever met.
   c. She received a citation for her bravery.
   d. No mistakes.

985. a. They have the arduous task of counting all the votes.
   b. Put the horses back in the corral.
   c. The door is falling off that dilapidated house.
   d. No mistakes.

986. a. Quincy is dyeing all his shirts purple.
   b. Did you get your tetinus shot?
   c. Timothy landed in the state penitentiary.
   d. No mistakes.

987. a. Let's search the premises.
   b. Due to the lack of rain, the reservoir is low.
   c. Is that a rhetorical question?
   d. No mistakes.

988. a. What is the tarrif on foreign car imports?
   b. The heart surgeon performed the delicate operation.
   c. I want to play in the chess tournament.
   d. No mistakes.

989. a. That corporation is subsidized by the government.
   b. There were several witnesses to the crime.
   c. Elizabeth Cady Stanton was part of the women's suffrage movement.
   d. No mistakes.

990. a. Without her guidence I would never have graduated.
   b. I am unable to ascertain the truth.
   c. That restaurant serves the best biscuits in town.
   d. No mistakes.

991. a. Homophones are words that sound alike but have different meanings.
b. I will definately have your television repaired by tomorrow.
c. Don't be so presumptuous!
d. No mistakes.

992. a. Your perception is not the same as mine.
b. Go to the personnel department and ask the human resources director.
c. We did a thorough investigation.
d. No mistakes.

993. a. The millionaire gave half of his fortune to charity.
b. I am writing a memoir about my travels.
c. I heard him mermuring that he was angry with you.
d. No mistakes.

994. a. He was forced to liquidate most of his assets.
b. No wonder the employees are complaining.
c. My insurance costs ninety-nine dollars a month.
d. No mistakes.

995. a. What an ignoramous!
b. What prompted you to accelerate?
c. Plagiarism is grounds for expulsion.
d. No mistakes.

996. a. You have already been inoculated against diphtheria.
b. Look in the bureau drawer.
c. Today in biology class we studied parisites.
d. No mistakes.

997. a. In his toolbox, he carried a screwdriver, a chisel, and a plane.
b. The chancellor gave the opening address.
c. He was more than apologetic.
d. No mistakes.

998. a. His attitude was cavalier, but I didn't mind.
b. The belegered firefighters battled the forest fire.
c. Judge Judy presided over the arraignment.
d. No mistakes.

999. a. We boiled water in a large cauldron.
b. You can see the exhibition at the county fairgrounds.
c. The duke and duchess waved at the crowd.
d. No mistakes.

1000. a. Charleen plays the saxophone, trumpet, and guitar.
b. It was an arduous task, but we completed it.
c. The financeer took all his money and went to live on a desert island.
d. No mistakes.

1001. a. Christopher has always thought of himself as a rennaisance man.
b. You will find them picnicking in the park.
c. Erica has always had a mischievous nature.
d. No mistakes.

ANSWERS

SECTION 1: SYNONYMS

SET 1 (Page 6)

1. **d.** *Enthusiastic* means eager or excited.
2. **a.** If something is *adequate*, it is sufficient.
3. **d.** A person who is *ecstatic* is thrilled or exhilarated.
4. **d.** To *affect* means to influence.
5. **c.** *Continuous* means marked by uninterrupted extension in space and time.
6. **a.** A *courtesy* implies being courteous or mannerly; it is civility.
7. **b.** A *frail* person is weak and delicate.
8. **a.** *Recuperate* means to heal; to mend.
9. **d.** *Sufficient* and *adequate* both mean enough.
10. **b.** If you gain your *composure*, you have poise.
11. **c.** An *eccentric* person is considered to be peculiar.
12. **a.** *Commendable* is the same as admirable.
13. **a.** *Passive* means not active.
14. **b.** *Vast* means very great in size; immense.
15. **d.** To *comply* is the same as to obey.

16. a. *Will* and *resolve* mean the same thing.

17. d. If you *enlighten* someone, you have taught them something.

18. a. If something is *rigorous,* it is demanding.

19. d. If you are *oblivious* to your surroundings, you are unaware of them.

20. b. To *verify* means to establish the truth or accuracy; to confirm.

21. d. A *rational* decision is a sound decision.

SET 2 (Page 8)

22. d. *Erroneous* mean inaccurate, faulty, or incorrect.

23. c. *Grotesque* means freakish, distorted, or hideous.

24. b. If something is *garbled,* it is jumbled or unintelligible.

25. c. If you *expose* something, you reveal it.

26. a. To *coerce* means to dominate by force.

27. b. *Abrupt* means sudden, quick, or hasty.

28. c. *Apathy* means a lack of interest or concern; indifference.

29. c. *Despair* means utter loss of hope.

30. c. A *contemptuous* person is full of scorn.

31. b. To *tote* means to carry.

32. d. If something is *distinct* it is distinguishable, or separate.

33. d. *Flagrant* means glaringly offensive.

34. c. An *oration* is a speech; an address.

35. d. *Libel* and *slander* both refer to defaming someone.

36. d. Philanthropy is a noun that means goodwill toward fellowmen; humanitarianism; generosity.

37. c. *Proximity* means the state of being proximate or near.

38. a. *Negligible* means of little consequence; insignificant.

39. b. *Vigilant* means watchful, especially to danger.

40. a. *Astute* and *perceptive* both mean having or showing a keen awareness.

41. a. To *collaborate* means to work jointly with others; to cooperate.

42. b. *Insipid* means lacking taste.

SET 3 (Page 10)

43. **c.** A *journal* and a *diary* are both records of daily happenings.

44. **c.** An *opportunity* to do something is the same as a *chance* to do it.

45. **b.** *Invent* means to create or to *discover*.

46. **c.** *Sphere* and *globe* both mean ball or orb.

47. **d.** To *refine* and to *purify* both mean to remove impurities.

48. **d.** *Pledge* and *promise* both mean a declaration that one will do something.

49. **d.** *Gangly* and *lanky* both mean tall, thin, and awkward.

50. **a.** *Sage* and *wise* both mean intelligent, perceptive.

51. **c.** To *navigate* and to *steer* both mean to direct a course.

52. **b.** *Dormant* and *slumbering* both mean sleeping.

53. **a.** To *banish* and to *exile* both mean to force to leave.

54. **d.** To *tailor* and to *alter* both mean to make something fit.

55. **b.** To *yield* and to *relinquish* both mean to give up.

56. **b.** To *croon* and to *vocalize* both mean to sing.

57. **a.** *Eternal* and *timeless* both mean without end.

58. **d.** A *hostel* and an *inn* are both lodging places.

59. **a.** To *stow* and to *pack* both mean to store away.

60. **b.** A *mesa* and a *plateau* are both hills with flat tops.

61. **d.** *Ado* and *fuss*, when used as nouns, both mean a hubbub or commotion.

62. **c.** *Intimate* and *private* both mean personal.

63. **a.** *Obscure* and *hidden* both mean concealed.

64. **d.** To *consider* and to *deem* both mean to regard as or to judge.

65. **a.** To *humidify* and to *moisten* both mean to make damp.

SET 4 (Page 12)

66. **c.** To *arouse* and to *waken* both mean to stir or to cause to become alert.

67. **a.** A *malicious* action and a *spiteful* action are both intended to harm.

68. **d.** To *harass* and to *humiliate* both mean to torment.

69. **a.** *Fortified* and *reinforced* both mean strengthened.

70. **d.** To *delegate* and to *assign* both mean to authorize or to appoint.

71. **d.** *Obsolete* and *outmoded* both mean no longer in use.

72. **a.** *Expansive* and *outgoing* both mean open and sociable.

73. **c.** To be held *accountable* and to be held *responsible* both mean to be held answerable for something.

74. **b.** *Philosophy* means a system of motivating *principles*.

75. **b.** A *custom* is a common practice; a *habit* is a practice followed regularly.

76. **c.** A *harbor* is a place of security; a *refuge* is a place that provides shelter or protection.

77. **b.** To *muse* and to *ponder* both mean to consider carefully or at length.

78. **a.** *Relinquish* means to let go or release; *abandon* means to desert.

79. **a.** A *vessel* and a *container* are both receptacles for holding goods.

80. **b.** *Submissively* means the state of submitting to others; *obediently* implies compliance.

81. **a.** *Ponderous* means unwieldy or clumsy because of weight or size.

82. **a.** *Stoically* means not showing passion or feeling; *impassively* means expressionless.

83. **c.** *Haggard* means having a worn or an emaciated appearance; *gaunt* means excessively thin.

84. **a.** To *dispute* is to engage in argument; to *debate* is to argue about.

85. **b.** An *enigma* is something hard to understand or explain; a mystery.

86. **d.** *Jocular* means given to jesting; habitually *jolly*.

87. **a.** To *rebuke* is to censure angrily; to *scold* is to reproach abusively.

88. **b.** *Renown* means a state of being honored; *fame* means popular acclaim.

SET 5 (Page 14)

89. d. *Robust* means showing vigor or strength.

90. a. *Site* means the place or spatial point of something; *location* means a position or place occupied or marked by some distinguishing feature.

91. b. *Mundane* means characterized by the practical and commonplace; *ordinary* means of a kind to be expected in the normal order of events.

92. d. *Compensate* means to make an appropriate payment to.

93. c. *Remiss* means showing neglect or inattention; *negligent* means not taking prudent care.

94. c. *Imminently* means in the near or immediate future; *soon* means in a prompt manner.

95. a. *Inordinately* means exceeding reasonable limits; *excessively* means going beyond a normal limit.

96. a. *Disheveled* means marked by disorder or disarray; *rumpled* means mussed up or tousled.

97. c. *Disillusioned* means the condition of being disenchanted or disappointed.

98. d. *Query* means to ask questions about to resolve a doubt; *inquire* means to ask about or search into.

99. d. *Clemency* means an act or instance of leniency; *mercy* means compassion shown to an offender.

100. a. *Attribute* means a characteristic or quality of a person or thing.

101. a. *Subdue* means to bring under control; conquer.

102. b. *Confer* means to compare views or to take counsel; consult with.

103. a. A *repast* is a meal; a *meal* is food served and eaten in one sitting.

104. b. To be *apathetic* is to show little emotion or interest; to be *indifferent* is to have no particular interest or concern.

105. b. To be *surreptitious* is to be clandestine or stealthy; to be *secretive* is to be covert.

106. d. To be *animated* is to be filled with vigor and activity; to be *lively* is to be full of energy or to be vigorous.

107. c. To *augment* is to increase or make greater in extent; to *expand* is to increase in size.

108. d. To be *incredulous* is to be skeptical; to be *disbelieving* is to refuse to believe in.

109. c. To be *vindictive* is to be vengeful; to be *spiteful* is to be malicious.

110. a. To be *menial* is to be servile; to be *lowly* is to be humble or plain.

111. a. A *panacea* is an all-compassing remedy; a *cure* is a remedy or restoration to health.

SET 6 (Page 16)

112. d. To be *glib* is to be quick or fluent in a way that suggests insincerity; to be *superficial* is to be shallow.

113. d. *Intricate* means having many complexly arranged elements; *complex* means complicated.

114. a. To be *cognizant* of something is to be aware of it; to be *conscious* of something is the same thing.

115. c. To *mediate* is to settle disputes; to *reconcile* is to bring into agreement.

116. b. *Concurrent* means happening at the same time; *simultaneous* means the same thing.

117. a. To *induce* is to bring about; to *prompt* is to provoke or induce to action.

118. d. To *manipulate* is to manage or to *handle* in a controlling manner.

119. c. To *saturate* is to fill or to load to capacity; to *soak* is to penetrate or permeate.

120. d. One of the meanings of to *proscribe* is to prohibit; to *forbid* is to command (someone) not to do something. *Proscribe* should not be confused with *prescribe*, which is what a doctor does with a medication.

121. a. To *refrain* is to hold back from doing something; to *desist* is to cease doing something.

122. d. A *domain* is an area governed by a ruler; a *territory* is an area for which someone is responsible.

123. a. To *escalate* is to increase in extent; to *intensify* is to make larger or stronger.

124. c. To be *urbane* is to show the refined manners of high society; to be *sophisticated* is to show worldly knowledge or refinement.

125. b. To *enumerate* means to ascertain the number of; to *count*.

126. d. To be *pertinacious* means to be stubbornly unyielding or *tenacious*.

127. c. To have an *aversion* to something means to have a feeling of repugnance for it or *dislike* of it.

128. a. To *validate* means to *confirm* the authenticity of something.

129. b. To have an *antagonist* is to have an *opponent*, or one who opposes you.

130. c. To have *perseverance* means to be steadfast in your course or to have *persistence*.

131. a. *Homogeneous* means of the same or a similar kind, *alike*.

132. d. A *recluse* is a person who lives withdrawn or shut up from the world, a *hermit*.

133. c. *Nevertheless* means nonetheless or in spite of, *however*.

134. b. *Placid* means serenely free of disturbance; calm, *peaceful*.

SET 7 (Page 18)

135. **c.** *Inferior* is lower in rank, quality, or importance.

136. **a.** *Curt* means in a rude or *gruff* manner.

137. **a.** *Perilous* means in a hazardous manner; dangerous.

138. **b.** *Precise* means exactly or sharply defined.

139. **a.** *Commence* means begin.

140. **d.** Someone who is *humble* is meek and non-assertive.

141. **b.** *Jubilant* means joyful.

142. **d.** A *replica* is a close reproduction; a copy or duplicate.

143. **a.** *Temperate* means not extreme or excessive; *moderate* means avoiding extremes of behavior or expression.

144. **a.** *Destitute* means lacking possessions and resources.

145. **b.** *Agile* means marked by ready ability to move with quick and easy grace; *nimble* means quick and light in motion.

146. **a.** *Brazenly* means marked by contemptuous boldness.

147. **c.** *Unique* means being the only one of its kind; *unparalleled* means unequaled.

148. **d.** To be a *prerequisite* is to be required; to be *required* is to be needed.

149. **a.** To *alleviate* is to make more bearable; to *ease* is to free from pain.

150. **d.** To be *inundated* is to be overwhelmed or swamped; to be *flooded* is to be submerged.

151. **a.** *Unanimous* means in complete assent or agreement; *uniform* means unvarying or the same as another or others.

152. **d.** To be *proficient* is to be expert or adept at something; to be *skilled* is to show ability or expertness.

153. **d.** *Obstinately* means refractory or stubborn; *stubbornly* means unduly determined, not easily persuaded.

154. **a.** To *rectify* is to set something right; to *correct* is to remove errors from something.

155. **c.** *Aspiration* means the same as *ambition*.

156. **c.** *Facet* means any of the definable aspects or details that make up a subject.

SET 8 (Page 20)

157. a. *Expedite* means accelerate the process; to speed up.

158. a. *Fortune* means luck or fate.

159. c. To *absolve* means to exonerate or forgive, to free from blame or responsibility.

160. d. *Hoist* means to raise.

161. d. *Predictable* means foreseeable.

162. c. To *shore up* means to prop up and support.

163. d. *Simmering* means barely controlled; seething.

164. b. To *initiate* means to begin or cause to begin.

165. c. *Ravenous* means voracious, all-consuming.

166. b. *Uninhabitable* implies conditions are so terrible that life cannot be sustained there.

167. b. *Suppressed* means held in, repressed, not expressed outwardly.

168. b. To be *immersed* in means to be absorbed, engrossed, or involved in profoundly.

169. a. *Secular* means worldly, not specifically pertaining to religion.

170. a. *Haggle* means to bargain or dicker.

171. d. A *palpable* tension is so intense it almost seems a physical, tangible presence.

172. c. One meaning of *vicarious* is to experience or realize something through imaginative or sympathetic participation.

173. c. One meaning of *sprawl* is haphazard growth of a city, usually outward toward the suburbs.

174. a. *Exotic* means foreign, intriguing, having the charm of the unfamiliar.

175. d. To *meander* means to follow a winding course.

176. b. *Precarious* means dangerous.

177. a. *Precocious* means characterized by early development or maturity of attitude and behavior.

178. a. A *quandary* refers to a dilemma or state of perplexity.

SET 9 (Page 22)

179. **a.** *Cite* means to mention in support of one's own statement or argument.

180. **b.** *Insatiable* means unquenchable or incapable of ever being satisfied.

181. **a.** A *nominal* sum is a trifling sum, one that is insignificantly small.

182. **c.** *Inhibited* means reverted, restrained, or held back.

183. **a.** The *essence* of something is the fundamental, essential part, the true meaning.

184. **d.** An *expletive* is an exclamation or oath, usually obscene or profane.

185. **a.** *Ripple* means gradually spreading or influencing.

186. **b.** A *rite* is a ceremonial act or action.

187. **d.** A *maverick* is a dissenter; one who refuses to abide by the dictates of the group.

188. **a.** *Mayhem* is wanton destruction, usually with the infliction of injury on another person. Mayhem may or may not involve killing (choice **c**).

189. **d.** To *neutralize* means to counteract or render inactive or ineffective.

190. **c.** A *shackle* is a restraint to further growth or action.

191. **c.** To *censure* means to criticize, blame, or incriminate, usually in some kind of formal way.

192. **a.** *Insufferable* means intolerable or incapable of being endured.

193. **b.** A *labyrinth* is a maze.

194. **a.** *Quintessence* means the purest instance or very essence.

195. **c.** *Consummate* means complete or perfect.

196. **c.** To *eclipse* means to overshadow or push another into obscurity by one's own more noticeable accomplishments.

197. **b.** A *hyperbole* is an extravagant statement, an exaggeration or overstatement.

198. **a.** A *proponent* is an advocate or supporter; someone who argues in favor of something.

199. **d.** To *disparage* is to talk about something or someone in a negative manner; to belittle.

200. **d.** To *apprise* means to tell; to *inform* means to communicate knowledge to.

SET 10 (Page 24)

201. b. To *scrutinize* is to examine carefully.

202. d. *Irrelevant* means not having significant bearing on the matter at hand; not essential.

203. c. *Rigidity* means an uncompromising inflexibility.

204. c. To be *magnanimous* means to be noble of mind or generous.

205. c. *Partisan* means exhibiting blind and prejudiced allegiance to something.

206. d. *Articulate* means to express clearly and effectively.

207. b. *Meticulous* means marked by extreme or excessive care; painstaking.

208. c. *Animosity* is a strong resentment or hostility toward something.

209. a. A *synopsis* is an abbreviated version; a *summary* is a brief statement of facts or points.

210. c. *Meager* means deficient in quality or quantity; thin; scanty.

211. c. *Noxious* means poisonous or harmful.

212. a. *Equity* means justice or impartiality.

213. b. *Affluence* means great wealth.

214. d. *Ominous* means foreshadowing evil, threatening.

215. a. To *defray* means to provide for the payment of something, to *pay*.

216. d. *Impromptu* means without preparation; *spontaneous* means unpremeditated.

217. b. A *statute* is a law.

218. b. Something that is *spurious* is not genuine.

219. a. To *emulate* a person means to strive to equal that person or to imitate that person.

220. b. An *idiosyncrasy* is a characteristic peculiarity or eccentricity.

221. b. *Penurious* means stingy or miserly.

222. c. Precognition means *clairvoyance*, the ability to foretell an occurrence without any objective evidence (sometimes called "second sight").

223. b. The *penumbra* is the partial shadow of an eclipse, between complete shadow and complete illumination.

224. c. *Circumspect* means careful or prudent in regard to one's own interests.

SET 11 (Page 26)

225. a. *Tactful* and *diplomatic* are synonyms (they mean about the same thing). *Bashful* and *timid* are also synonyms. The answer is not **b** or **c** because neither of these means the same as *bashful*. Bold (choice **d**) is incorrect because it means the opposite of *bashful*.

226. a. If someone has been *humiliated,* they have been greatly *embarrassed.* If someone is *terrified,* they are extremely *frightened.* The answer is not **b** because an agitated person is not necessarily frightened. Choices **c** and **d** are incorrect because neither word expresses a state of being frightened.

227. a. *Control* and *dominate* are synonyms, and *magnify* and *enlarge* are synonyms.

228. b. *Exactly* and *precisely* are synonyms, and *evidently* and *apparently* are synonyms. Choices **a, c,** and **d** are incorrect because none mean the same as apparently.

229. a. *Neophyte* and *novice* mean the same thing. *Pursuit* and *quest* are synonyms. The other choices do not mean pursuit.

230. a. *Regard* and *esteem* mean the same thing. *Ambivalence* and *uncertainty* are synonyms. The other choices do not mean ambivalence.

231. b. *Restrain* and *curb* are synonyms. *Retract* means the same thing as *recant.* The other choices do not mean recant.

232. d. *Capricious* means the same thing as *whimsical.* *Shrewd* and *astute* are synonyms. The other choices do not mean the same as shrewd.

233. c. *Obstinate* and *stubborn* are synonyms. *Staunch* and *faithful* mean the same thing. The other choices do not mean the same as staunch.

234. a. *Resolutely* and *perseveringly* mean the same thing. *Spuriously* and *falsely* are synonyms. The other choices do not mean the same as spuriously.

235. b. *Hypocrite* and *phony* are synonyms. *Lethargy* and *stupor* mean the same thing. The other choices do not mean the same as lethargy.

236. c. *Component* and *constituent* are synonyms. *Epoch* and *era* mean the same thing. The other choices do not mean the same as epoch.

237. d. *Dupe* and *deceive* mean the same thing. *Exculpate* and *absolve* are synonyms. The other choices do not mean the same as exculpate.

238. a. *Heterogeneous* and *mixed* are synonyms. *Profuse* and *lush* mean the same thing. The other choices do not mean the same as profuse.

239. b. *Disclose* and *reveal* are synonyms. *Imitate* and *copy* mean the same thing. The other choices do not mean the same as imitate.

240. c. *Conceal* and *obscure* mean the same thing. *Procrastinate* and *delay* are synonyms. The other choices do not mean the same as procrastinate.

241. a. *Futilely* and *vainly* are synonyms. *Covertly* and *secretly* mean the same thing. The other choices do not mean the same as covertly.

242. d. *Opposing* and *differing* are synonyms. *Candid* and *frank* mean the same thing. The other choices do not mean the same as candid.

243. b. *Expeditiously* and *swiftly* are synonyms. *Diligently* and *persistently* mean the same thing. The other choices do not mean the same as diligently.

SET 12 (Page 28)

244. b. full of
245. d. opposite of or contrary to
246. a. state or quality
247. d. again or anew
248. b. partial or partially
249. c. over or above
250. c. condition, state, or quality
251. d. three
252. b. like or resembling
253. b. opposing or against
254. a. undo
255. c. between or among
256. a. together
257. d. to fasten
258. c. before or prior to
259. d. above or over
260. c. both
261. b. new or recent
262. b. completely, intensely
263. a. below, under
264. b. push
265. a. hear

SET 13 (Page 30)

266. b. mind, mental
267. c. all
268. d. action or process of
269. b. having the qualities of
270. a. to cause to be or to become
271. c. tending toward
272. a. thoroughly
273. b. air
274. b. bad or abnormal
275. d. other or different
276. c. light
277. a. place for
278. c. out of
279. d. large
280. b. state or quality
281. b. back or backward
282. d. many
283. a. science or study
284. c. speech or discourse
285. a. process
286. b. hidden or secret
287. c. muscle

SET 14 (Page 32)

288. **c.** Examples: I love my little *dog* Boopsy. The police had begun to *dog* us everywhere we went.

289. **b.** Examples: A *crow* landed among the cornstalks. That award was something to *crow* about!

290. **a.** Examples: I love to walk in that *field* and smell the buttercups. Computer Science is not my *field*.

291. **c.** Examples: My favorite *film* is *The Mummy's Curse*. There was a *film* of grease over everything in the kitchen.

292. **c.** Examples: The burglars put a *gag* over the store-owner's mouth. I put a beetle in my brother's soup as a *gag*.

293. **d.** Examples: My hair was *medium* brown before I colored it red. The *medium* summoned up the spirit of my dead Uncle Elmer.

294. **a.** Examples: I'd rather play *pool* than go to class. Cindy Crawford invited us to swim in her *pool*.

295. **c.** Examples: The wisest political course is often the *mean* between two extremes. My Uncle Clarence was a *mean* penny-pincher until the day he died.

296. **d.** Examples: Sally Sue got a new *dolly* for her birthday. We'll need a *dolly* to unload all those crates of sausage off the truck.

297. **a.** Examples: When my father began to speak, the room grew very *still*. I took care of my brother-in-law's moonshine *still* while he was in jail.

298. **d.** Examples: Big Bart likes to *strut* around town in his logging boots. A slender pine-wood *strut* kept the scarecrow from falling over.

299. **b.** Examples: The overall growth in the economy caused business to *boom* in our town. While trying out his new sailboat, my friend Robert was hit in the head with the *boom* and knocked into the sea.

300. **c.** Examples: "City Slicker" is a really *fast* horse. A good way to diet is to *fast* one day a week.

301. **a.** Examples: Aunt Nell played the church *organ* for forty years. An *organ* transplant can often save a life.

302. **b.** Examples: The *frame* of the old cabin is still standing. Lefty was able to *frame* Big Louie for the heist.

303. **c.** Examples: My Algebra teacher was very *stern*, and we were all frightened of her. The H.M.S. *Argonaut* was gorgeous from stem to *stern*.

304. **a.** Examples: Vladimir was a real *rake*, but all the women loved him. I will use my new *rake* to make my lawn look neat and tidy.

305. **b.** Examples: They served lamb *curry*, which made me sick. The soldiers tried to *curry* favor with the lieutenant.

306. **d.** Examples: All we did that summer was lie around reading trashy *pulp* fiction. Scoop out the *pulp* of the apricot and mix it with powdered sugar.

SECTION 2: VOCABULARY IN CONTEXT

SET 15 (Page 36)

307. **d.** The word *problem* in this context means a source of distress. Choices **b** and **c** do not make sense. Choice **a** is a great source of distress, but parking tickets are usually not a disaster.

308. **c.** *Rescue* in this context implies freeing from danger. The other choices do not make sense.

309. **a.** *Consider* means to think about carefully.

310. **b.** The context clue is "we knew nothing." *Secretive* means having the habit of keeping secrets.

311. **b.** *Summit* means the highest point, where the hikers would have a view.

312. **c.** A *consequence* is the result of something.

313. **c.** A *musty* odor is one that is stale or moldy. The other choices are not descriptive of an odor.

314. **a.** *Solitude*, unlike *loneliness* (choice **c**), can be a desirable thing. It's doubtful that a person who dealt with *crowds of noisy, demanding people* every day would want *association* (choice **b**). Choice **d** makes no sense.

315. **b.** To be *shunned* is to be avoided deliberately, usually as a punishment.

316. **c.** Bobby's acting up in class must have made Ms. Willy angry (*irate*) or she probably would not have thrown an eraser. Although she was certainly *animated* (choice **a**) and although throwing an eraser is *incautious* (**b**), these words do not imply anger. Choice **d** makes no sense.

317. **a.** *Spiteful* means filled with hate or malice.

318. **a.** *Accessible* means capable of being reached; being within reach.

319. **d.** *Outmoded* means no longer in style or no longer usable.

320. **b.** A *quest* is a search or pursuit of something.

321. **d.** *Ingenious* means marked by originality, resourcefulness, and cleverness in conception; clever.

322. **c.** To be *indispensable* is to be essential or necessary.

323. **d.** *Chronic* means habitually reccurring.

324. **b.** *Adversely* means acting against or in a contrary direction.

SET 16 (Page 38)

325. d. *Docile* means easily led or managed.

326. c. *Explicit* means clearly defined.

327. b. *Apathetic* means having little or no concern. (The principal had expected an uproar, but that never happened.)

328. d. *Potable* means fit for drinking.

329. a. *Encompasses* in this context means includes.

330. a. *Devised* means to form in the mind by new combinations or applications of ideas or principles; to plan to obtain or bring about.

331. d. To *intimidate* means to make timid or fearful; to frighten.

332. c. *Quandary* means a state of perplexity or doubt.

333. a. *Precedence* means priority of importance— i.e., studying is more important to Jessica than watching the Academy Awards.

334. c. *Conspicuous* means obvious to the eye or mind; attracting attention.

335. a. *Monotonous* means having a tedious sameness.

336. d. *Resolved* means having reached a firm decision about something.

337. a. *Portrayal* means representation or portrait.

338. c. *Careen* means to rush headlong or carelessly; to lurch or swerve while in motion.

339. a. *Pungent* implies a sharp, stinging, or biting quality, especially of odor.

340. d. *Audibly* means heard or the manner of being heard.

341. b. *Voraciously* means having a huge appetite; ravenously.

342. a. *Mishap* means an unfortunate accident.

SET 17 (Page 40)

343. **d.** *Legitimately* means in a manner conforming to recognized principles or accepted rules or standards.

344. **a.** *Warily* means in a manner marked by keen caution, cunning, and watchful prudence. The context clue in this sentence is Jeffrey's nervousness.

345. **b.** *Coyly* means in a manner that is marked by cute, coquettish, or artful playfulness. In this context, the other choices make no sense.

346. **a.** *Arrogant* means exaggerating or disposed to exaggerate one's own worth or importance in an overbearing manner.

347. **a.** *Wanton* means being without check or limitation.

348. **d.** *Integrity* means firm adherence to a code of moral values; honesty.

349. **b.** To *pummel* means to pound or beat.

350. **a.** An *eccentricity* something that deviates from the norm. (Antique lemon juicers are not a commonplace item.)

351. **b.** *Respite* means an interval of rest and relief.

352. **d.** *Facilitate* means to make easier or help to bring about.

353. **c.** *Exemplify* means to be an instance of or serve as an example.

354. **b.** *Confluence* means a coming or flowing together, meeting, or gathering at one point.

355. **d.** *Requisite* means essential or necessary.

356. **a.** *Delude* means to mislead the mind; to deceive.

357. **c.** *Comprehensive* means covering completely or broadly. (*Massive*, choice **d**, refers to a large or bulky mass.)

358. **b.** *Reticent* means inclined to be silent or uncommunicative; reserved. Mary was silent at first, but then talked more than anyone else.

359. **b.** *Precursor* means something that comes before.

360. **b.** *Reputedly* means according to general belief.

SET 18 (Page 42)

361. a. *Abated* means to decrease in force or intensity.

362. c. *Consummate* means extremely skilled and experienced.

363. c. *Assiduously* means in a careful manner or with unremitting attention.

364. d. A *commentary* is something that explains or illustrates and fits best in this context.

365. b. To *poach* is to trespass on another's property in order to steal fish or game. Choices **a** and **c** would make little sense. Choice **d** seems too grand a description for the actions of two small boys.

366. d. To *differentiate* between two things is to establish the distinction between them. The other choices, although somewhat related, make no sense.

367. a. Something *squalid* has a dirty or wretched appearance. The other adjectives, though somewhat related, can properly be applied to a person but not to a place.

368. b. When a car goes out of control and skims along the surface of a wet road, it is called *hydroplaning.*

369. d. A clairvoyant is someone who can perceive matters beyond the range of ordinary perception.

370. a. The word *unearthly* (frighteningly weird and unnatural) best describes the way a ghost might *shriek.* A *shriek* cannot be *covert* (hidden, choice **b**), nor can it be *abstruse* (difficult to understand, choice **c**) because it does not seek to explain anything. The word *esoteric* (known only to a small number) does not precisely apply to a *shriek*, either.

371. d. A *vortex* is a whirlpool and so fits the sentence. The other choices do not make sense.

372. d. To be *recalcitrant* is to be stubbornly resistant. The other adjectives are not usually applied to human beings.

373. b. To be *feasible* is to be practicable and so the word best fits this sentence. The other three choices would not apply to projects that are possible (note that they all begin with prefixes generally meaning "not").

374. b. Something that is *iridescent* displays lustrous, rainbow colors. Choices **a** and **b** are somewhat close, but neither includes color as a necessary property. *Cumulous* (choice **d**) is a scientific name for a type of cloud.

375. c. To have *rapport* is to have mutual trust and emotional affinity. The other words do not necessarily imply trust.

376. d. A *strident* voice is one that is loud, harsh, and grating, so it best fits the sentiment "sit down and shut up." The word *clamorous* (choice **a**) has the connotation of a public outcry in more than one voice. *Flocculent* (choice **b**) denotes something fluffy or woolly, and *affable* (choice **c**) means "amiable."

377. d. To be *reticent* is to be disinclined to speak out. The other choices make no sense in this context.

378. c. To *retract* something is to take it back or disavow it. This is the term usually applied to disavowing something erroneous or libelous printed in a newspaper. The other choices are somewhat similar in meaning but do not normally apply to newspaper errors.

379. c. If something is *incontrovertible*, it is irrefutable. This word makes most sense in the context of an obvious crime.

SET 19 (Page 44)

380. a. To *administer* means to give something remedially (transitive verb). To *minister* means to aid or give service to people (intransitive verb).

381. a. *Eager* implies enthusiastic or impatient desire or interest. *Anxious* implies a more negative feeling: an extreme uneasiness of mind, or worried.

382. a. *Ensure* means to make a future occurrence certain or reliable; *insure* means protecting the worth of goods; *assure* means to promise or cause someone to count on.

383. b. *Nauseated* means to feel nausea or the condition of feeling sick. *Nauseous* means causing nausea; nauseating; sickening. If you say you are nauseous it means you have unpleasant powers.

384. b. *Well* should be used as an adverb to modify verbs (how does it fit?). *Good* is an adjective often used with linking verbs (be, seem, or appear).

385. b. *Comprises* means to consist of—it expresses the relation of the larger to the smaller (think of this larger sense by remembering that *comprises* is a longer word than *composes*). *Composes* means to make up the parts of.

386. a. *Discomfit* means to wholly undo or defeat. *Discomfort* means to deprive of comfort or to distress.

387. a. *Credible* means offering reasonable grounds for being believed; *credulous* means ready to believe, especially on slight or uncertain evidence.

388. a. *Annoy* means a wearing on the nerves by persistent petty unpleasantness; *aggravate* means to make worse, more serious, or more severe—to intensify unpleasantly.

389. a. *Adapt* implies a modification according to changing circumstances. *Adopt* means accepting something created by another or foreign to one's nature.

390. b. *Healthful* implies a positive contribution to a healthy condition, or beneficial to health. *Healthy* implies full of strength and vigor as well as freedom from signs of disease.

391. b. *Induct* means to introduce or initiate. *Deduct* means to take away from a total.

392. a. *Exhaustive* means treating all parts without omission. *Exhausting* means tiring.

393. a. *Feasible* means logical or likely. *Possible* means capable of happening or existing.

394. b. *Continuously* means uninterrupted in time. *Continually* means recurring regularly.

395. a. *Proceed* means to go forward in an orderly way; *precede* means to come before.

396. a. *Counsel* means advice or guidance. A *council* is an assembly of people called together for consultation.

397. b. *Compulsory* means obligatory or required. *Compulsive* means having the capacity to compel.

398. b. *Judicious* is having or exhibiting sound judgment. *Judicial* is of or relating to courts of law.

399. a. *Tortuous* means winding or twisting. *Torturous* means of, relating to, or causing torture.

SET 20 (Page 46)

400. **d.** be forgotten
401. **a.** set or ask a price of
402. **a.** a complete course, succession, or series (Note that choice **b** is the wrong part of speech.)
403. **a.** mind and emotions as distinguished from the physical body (Choice **b** may be tempting, but the usual colloquial meaning of the phrase *with us in spirit* is choice **a.**)
404. **d.** instance or example (Choices **a** and **b** are superficially attractive, but the phrase *case of mistaken identity* can be used without reference to a claim or legal action.)
405. **a.** caused to move in a given direction
406. **c.** slight trace or bit
407. **b.** flagrant
408. **c.** to wash against with a gentle slapping sound
409. **a.** formulate
410. **c.** official routes of communication
411. **d.** glaze
412. **a.** prepare for action (note that choices **c** and **d** are not the correct parts of speech to fit grammatically)
413. **c.** squarely or solidly (note that choice **a** is the wrong part of speech)
414. **d.** incline
415. **c.** react explosively

SET 21 (Page 48)

416. **c.** lame (note that choice **b** is the wrong part of speech)
417. **b.** impudence or effrontery
418. **c.** two persons or things that harmonize with each other (We can assume that Clarissa and Calvin are people, which is the clue to choice **c.**)
419. **d.** is not concerned or troubled
420. **d.** device for circulating air
421. **b.** an arrangement in an orderly series
422. **d.** break away from
423. **a.** fellow
424. **b.** equivocate
425. **b.** extensive area of open land
426. **c.** body of official advisors
427. **b.** set at a specified downward slant
428. **b.** sell pilfered (stolen) goods
429. **d.** water pump
430. **c.** a preliminary sketch, outline, or version
431. **a.** to describe as having a specified character or quality

SET 22 (Page 50)

432. b. The word *pristine* is more a precise word for fresh and clean.

433. d. *Gaggle* is the most precise and interesting word. *Herd* (choice **b**) does not apply to birds.

434. b. To *savor* means to taste or smell with pleasure.

435. a. *Abruptly* means unexpectedly, occurring without warning.

436. c. *Script* refers to a specific way of forming letters.

437. d. The word *dingy* helps us picture the hallway better than the other choices do.

438. c. *Yank* is the only choice that fits the context of the sentence.

439. b. The word *immaculate* is the only one that connotes cleanliness.

440. d. *Dissuade* means to advise a person against something. Choices **a** and **b** make no sense. Choice **c** changes the meaning of the sentence.

441. d. This gives the most precise picture of the way the little girls moved and creates a visual image of moving in circles. *Rotated* (choice **a**) is an attractive choice, but is generally not used to refer to dancing.

442. b. This is the most vivid and zany exclamation, befitting a person who is on his third martini.

443. a. *Debilitated* means weakened or enfeebled.

444. c. This is the most succinct, accurate description, and the only one that includes the element of *disorder*.

445. c. *Convoy* means a group organized for protection in moving.

446. d. *Bustled*, meaning moved briskly, is the only choice that gives an active picture of how Mom came into the room.

SET 23 (Page 52)

447. d. This is the only choice that makes sense within the context of the sentence.

448. b. A *squabble* is a quarrel and a more precise word than disagreement.

449. c. This is the only choice that fits the context of the sentence. *Lurch* indicates a jerking or swaying movement.

450. d. This is the only verb that gives us a concrete mental image of the way her hair looked. *Crimped* means to form into a desired shape.

451. a. This is the only adjective that gives us a picture of the rather silly, affected way she walked. The other choices are redundant.

452. c. *Consumed* means to do away with completely. The other choices make no sense.

453. b. This description is most specific. *Nutriment* (choice **a**) is not specific; choices **c** and **d** make no sense.

454. a. *Scintillate* means to emit quick flashes.

455. d. The word *jumble* is most descriptive of exactly how the furniture was piled; it helps us form a mental image better than the other choices do.

456. b. This choice is more concrete than the others and is the only one that describes an attitude toward the chiffonier.

457. d. *Jutted* is the most vivid and concrete of the choices, helping us picture how the envelope looked.

458. c. This is the most particular description of what the women were wearing, and helps us form a word picture.

459. a. *Ecstatic,* which means being in a state of overwhelming delight, is the only choice that makes sense.

460. a. *Surly* means irritably sullen in mood or manner. This is the only choice that indicates unfriendliness.

461. b. The word *miasma* connotes a poisonous vapor, an image that fits a state of depression. The other choices have other connotations and do not fit the context of the sentence.

SET 24 (Page 54)

462. **b.** A *grimace* is the contortion of facial features.

463. **d.** It makes sense that a subordinate monkey would be intimidated by a dominant one (choice **d**), and not the other way around (choice **b**). A monkey that is *calm* (choice **a**) would not be apt to show a *fear grimace*, nor would a monkey who is *confident* (choice **c**).

464. **b.** *Stout* works best in the context. Choice **a** can be ruled out because thin contradicts large. Choice **c** is redundant. There is no context to suggest choice **d**.

465. **b.** The author is describing Reed's appearance (in what is obviously an old-fashioned style). The word *spacious* means large or vast; the word *visage* means face.

466. **a.** An *extremity* is the outermost portion of something. The boy's *limbs* (arms and legs) have already been mentioned, so *hands and feet* is the next most logical choice.

467. **c.** *Askance* means with disapproval or distrust; scornfully. The context clue is the word *glared*, which indicates Leo's disapproval.

468. **c.** The immediate context of this adjective contains the words *luxury, burst, fire* and *gold*, all of which connote radiance.

469. **a.** Mention of *pine* immediately before the phrase and *new hay* immediately after makes choice **a,** *a plant*, the most logical choice.

470. **c.** Night usually brings darkness. There is no mention of death or ghosts (choice **a**) in the passage. The words *obscurity* and *indistinctness* (choices **b** and **d**) do not make sense here.

471. **c.** Debris and radiation are both *hazards;* choice **c** is the only possible answer.

472. **a.** *Muscle atrophy* and *bone loss* are examples of physical deterioration. There is no mention of

illness in the passage (choice **b**), and choices **c** and **d** do not have anything directly to do with muscles or bones.

473. **b.** Although a muscle that atrophies may be weakened (choice **c**), the primary meaning of the phrase *to atrophy* is *to waste away*.

474. **b.** The word *ambiance* refers to the distinctive atmosphere surrounding a person or place.

475. **a.** In the context of today's business world, an *entrepreneurial* business is one that is unique and a bit off center, so the word *idiosyncratic* fits best.

476. **a.** This choice fits best as a contrast to the words *small or medium* and *little*.

477. **b.** The whole passage describes destruction by a storm, a force of nature. Choices **a, c,** and **d** refer to destruction by human beings.

478. **a.** In this context, leveled means flattened or completely destroyed. The context clue here is the word *waterspouts*, which refers to tornadoes.

479. **b.** Choices **a, c,** and **d** are human reactions and traits; therefore, choice **b** is the most logical choice.

480. **d.** The context clue is the word *ancestors*, which indicates *generations*. Choices **a** and **b** are too short a period of time; choice **c** is impossible.

481. **c.** The word *shiftless* means lazy. The passage also speaks of Howard Carpenter's *callow fancy* and calls him *idle*. Choices **a** and **d** are too positive, choice **b** too negative for the context of the passage.

482. **a.** Neither choice **b** or choice **d** are mentioned in the passage. Choice **c** is mentioned, but does not encompass all the cowbird's behavior. Choice **a** is the most inclusive definition.

483. **a.** The word *lays* is the key here. The only thing a bird would lay would be a collection of eggs.

484. **d.** To *eject* something is to throw it out forcefully.

SET 25 (Page 59)

485. b. The word *option* means *choice*. The mention of *on-site* and *off-site* disposal denotes two choices for hospital waste disposal. The other options may be accurate but do not contain the element of choice.

486. a. The passage states that the preliminary processing *reduces the total volume* of solid wastes before it leaves hospital grounds. The other choices are not in the passage.

487. a. To consolidate matter is to form it into a *compact* mass. The other choices have very different meanings.

488. a. A *flag* is a symbol or emblem that stands in the place of a country. Given that fact, the other choices do not make sense.

489. b. The passage is about the day Ghana gained its independence. To be independent is to be *autonomous*. The other choices do not denote independence. Choice **a** may seem correct at first, but to be alone implies isolation, not necessarily independence.

490. b. *Dexterity* means skill with the use of the hands.

491. a. The fact that the passage is a *warning* points to choice **a**, which speaks of *adverse effects*. The other choices would not call for a warning.

492. d. To be allergic to a thing is to be sensitive to it. The other choices do not make sense in the context of the passage.

493. b. This choice, which means random or haphazard, makes most sense in the context of the passage. The use of medical abbreviations could not be choice **a**, *clandestine* (secret). The passage does not indicate that anything *unlawful* (choice **c**) is involved. The word *intrepid* (choice **d**) means fearless, which does not make sense in terms of the passage.

494. d. It is logical to deduce that unclear orders by a doctor, in the form of medical abbreviations, would call for clarification. The other choices are illogical.

495. b. The first sentence of the passage says that *adolescents* can be *BOTH victims and perpetrators*, so choice **a** is obviously wrong. Choices **c** and **d** are wrong because neither describes adolescents.

496. **c.** Since the passage deals with violence by and against adolescents, it makes most sense that *violence prevention programs* would attempt to teach peaceful settlement.

497. **d.** To *retaliate* means to get even, or pay back.

498. **b.** *Chalky* is a descriptive word often used in place of the word white. Eggs are not made of chalk (choices **a** and **d**), and there is nothing in the passage to suggest that anyone tasted the Albatross egg (choice **c**).

499. **c.** The *wake* is the turbulent water behind the ship, so choice **c** is the only logical choice. The other choices deal with other parts of a ship.

500. **c.** The main topic of the passage is the need for detectives to be *sensitive* to the fact that, for victims of crime, this is not an ordinary situation; therefore, the choice that contains the word insensitive makes the most sense in the context of the passage. Also the passage concerns detectives who *routinely* investigate violent crime— that is, have continued exposure to it, as stated in choice **c**.

501. **a.** Something that is *paradoxical* is contradictory. The phrase *in contrast* is the only term that is close in meaning.

502. **b.** The word *vulnerable* means "susceptible to injury," so choice **b** makes the most sense. Although the victims of violent crime may feel the emotions described in all the choices, a further clue to choice **b** is the statement that the victims of violent crime usually feel *violated*.

503. **d.** The topic of the passage is the need for detectives to be sensitive to the needs of the victims, so choice **d**, which contains the word *sympathetically*, fits best in context.

SET 26 (Page 63)

504. b. too
505. a. respect
506. d. follow
507. a. law
508. c. stop
509. b. wrong
510. b. disobey
511. b. believe
512. c. change
513. b. give
514. d. unjust
515. d. until
516. a. citizen
517. c. defied
518. c. break
519. b. inconvenient
520. a. listen
521. a. then
522. c. hearts
523. b. duty

SET 27 (Page 65)

524. a. bring
525. d. lives
526. b. effectively
527. a. of
528. c. extremes
529. b. when
530. b. answer
531. d. high
532. a. typical
533. c. faced
534. d. violate
535. b. or
536. a. investigation
537. c. outweighed
538. c. choice
539. b. corruption
540. d. result
541. d. cost
542. a. betrayed
543. b. eventually

SECTION 3: ANTONYMS

SET 28 (Page 68)

544. c. *Prompt* means *punctual*; *tardy* means *late*.

545. b. To *delay* is to *slow*; to *hasten* is to *hurry*.

546. c. To *soothe* is to *comfort*; to *aggravate* is to *irritate*.

547. d. *Moderate* means *average*; *excessive* means *extreme*.

548. d. To *reveal* is to *disclose*; to *conceal* is to *hide*.

549. c. *Initial* means *first*; *final* means *last*.

550. a. *Brittle* means *breakable*; *flexible* means *pliable*.

551. a. *Capable* means *able*; *unskilled* means *unable*.

552. a. To *stray* is to *wander*; to *remain* is to *stay*.

553. b. *Dainty* means *delicate*; *coarse* means *indelicate*.

554. d. *Craving* means *desire*; *repugnance* means *aversion*.

555. a. *Ferocious* means *savage*; *docile* means *tame*.

556. a. *Grueling* means *exhausting*; *effortless* means *easy*.

557. d. To *forsake* is to *abandon*; to *cherish* is to *nurture*.

558. b. To *restrain* is to *control*; to *liberate* is to *release*.

559. c. To be *bleak* is to be *dreary*; to be *bright* is to be *brilliant*.

SET 29 (Page 70)

560. a. *Unruly* means not easily managed, controlled, or disciplined; *controllable* is the opposite.

561. b. To be *alert* is to be *attentive*; to be *inattentive* is to be *unwatchful*.

562. b. *Solidarity* means *union*; *disunity* means *division*.

563. a. To *retract* is to *withdraw*; to *assert* is to *affirm*.

564. b. *Brief* means short; *lengthy* means long.

565. d. *Omit* means to leave out; *include* means to take in.

566. d. *Cautious* means prudent and discreet; *reckless* is the opposite of cautious.

567. b. *Prohibit* means to forbid; *permit* means to allow.

568. b. *Disclose* means to reveal; *conceal* means to prevent disclosure.

569. a. *Shameful* means dishonorable, so *honorable* is the opposite of shameful.

570. c. *Vague* means not clearly definite; *definite* means clearly defined.

571. a. *Stifle* means to discourage or smother; *encourage* is the opposite.

572. b. To *belittle* means to *criticize*, which is the opposite of *compliment*.

573. c. *Aimless* means lacking in purpose; *purposeful* means having an aim or purpose.

574. c. *Vulnerable* means open to attack or weak; *strong* is the opposite of weak.

575. a. *Distress* means subject to great strain, upset; *comfort* means calmness and peace.

SET 30 (Page 72)

576. a. *Unity* means harmony or compatibility; *discord* means a lack of harmony.

577. d. *Detest* means to feel hostility toward, to strongly dislike; the opposite of detest is *admire*.

578. b. *Valiant* means acting with bravery or boldness; *cowardly* is the opposite.

579. d. *Lenient* means permissive, tolerant, or easygoing; *domineering* means exercising overbearing control.

580. c. *Tarnish* means to destroy the luster of; *shine* means to make bright by polishing.

581. c. *Mandatory* means containing a command; *optional* means having a choice.

582. c. *Chagrin* means distress caused by disappointment or failure; *pleasure* is the opposite of distress.

583. d. *Commence* means to begin; *terminate* means to end.

584. a. *Conscientious* means careful, cautious, and thoughtful; *careless* means not showing care.

585. b. *Deficient* means lacking some necessary quality; *complete* means having all necessary parts.

586. c. *Clarify* means to make clear; *obscure* means to make dark, dim, or indistinct.

587. a. To *grant* is to permit; to *deny* is to refuse to permit.

588. d. *Lucid* means clear.

589. b. *Impartial* means not partial or biased; *prejudiced* means biased.

590. c. *Judicious* means wise or prudent; *imprudent* means not prudent.

591. a. *Dissonance* means not in harmony.

592. a. *Erudite* means learned or possessing knowledge; *uneducated* means to lack training or knowledge.

SET 31 (Page 74)

593. c. *Requirement* means something obligatory; *option* means something chosen.

594. a. To *irritate* means to annoy; to *soothe* means to calm.

595. d. To be *punctual* means to be on time; to be *tardy* means to be late.

596. c. *Virtue* means a moral goodness; *vice* means a moral failing.

597. d. *Harmony* means agreement; *discord* means disagreement.

598. a. An *insult* is a gross indignity; a *compliment* is an admiring remark.

599. a. *General* means not limited to one class of things; *specific* means particular.

600. b. To be *fortunate* is to have good luck; to be *hapless* is to be unlucky.

601. d. *Imaginary* means unreal; *factual* means real.

602. c. To *demolish* means to tear apart; to *create* means to build.

603. d. *Notable* means unusual; *ordinary* means usual.

604. a. *Prim* means stiffly formal and proper; *outrageous* means shocking.

605. b. *Prosperous* means rich or affluent; *destitute* means very poor.

606. b. *Absorb* means to take in or consume; to *repel* is to reject or force away.

607. d. To be *critical* is to be important or vital to something; to be *trivial* is to be unimportant.

608. b. *Nimble* means quick and light in motion; *sluggish* means slow or inactive.

609. a. *Tranquil* means peaceful; *agitated* means disturbed or excited.

610. c. *Sprightly* means lively; *dully* suggests a lack or loss of keenness or zest.

611. c. *Infantile* means childish; *mature* means grown up.

612. d. To be *impulsive* is to be swayed by emotion or to make rash decisions; to be *cautious* is to show forethought.

613. c. *Amiable* means friendly; the opposite of friendly is *aloof*.

614. c. *Competent* means having adequate abilities; *inept* means incapable or not competent.

615. b. To *promote* is to advance someone to a higher rank or to advocate something; to *curtail* is to cut something short.

SET 32 (Page 76)

616. **a.** To be *prudent* is to exercise good judgment; to be *rash* is to show ill-considered haste.

617. **b.** To *retain* is to keep or hold; to *release* is to let go.

618. **c.** *Scant* is meager; *copious* is abundant.

619. **b.** To be *steadfast* is to be fixed or unchanging; to be *fickle* is to be capricious.

620. **b.** To be *stringent* is to be rigorous or severe; to be *lax* is to be lacking in rigor or strictness.

621. **c.** To be *subjective* is to be influenced by one's own emotions or beliefs without strict regard to evidence in the outside world; to be *unbiased* is to be objective or impartial.

622. **d.** To be *succinct* is to be concise; to be *verbose* is to be wordy.

623. **a.** To be *tedious* is to be tiresome; to be *stimulating* is to be exciting.

624. **b.** To be *uniform* is to be consistent or the same as another or others; to be *diverse* is to have variety.

625. **d.** To be *wary* is to be on guard or watchful; *careless* is the opposite of watchful.

626. **d.** The adjective *novel* means new or not representing something formerly known; the adjective *old* means having lived or existed for a long time.

627. **a.** A *fallacy* is a false or mistaken idea, or trickery; a *truth* is something which conforms to the facts.

628. **d.** To *exonerate* means to clear from accusation or guilt; to *blame* is to accuse.

629. **d.** *Subsequent* means coming after or following; *previous* means coming before.

630. **c.** To be *nonchalant* means to have an air of easy indifference; to be *concerned* means to be interested and involved.

631. **b.** To *excise* means to remove; to *retain* means to keep.

632. **a.** To *disperse* means to scatter; to *gather* means to collect in one place.

633. **b.** *Prevarication* means evasion of the truth; *veracity* means truthfulness.

634. **b.** *Mirth* means merriment; *solemnity* means seriousness.

635. **b.** To *liberate* means to release; to *restrain* means to deprive of liberty.

636. **a.** *Faltering* means stumbling; *steady* means unfaltering.

637. **c.** *Optimum* means the most desirable; *worst* means the least desirable.

638. **b.** *Ephemeral* means short-lived; *enduring* means without end.

SET 33 (Page 78)

639. **a.** To *orient* means to adjust to; to *confuse* means to mix up.

640. **d.** To *levitate* means to rise and float; to *sink* means to go under the surface.

641. **c.** To *pacify* means to calm; to *excite* means to stir up.

642. **c.** To be *plausible* is to be likely; to be *unbelievable* is to be unlikely.

643. **b.** *Avidly* means characterized by enthusiasm and vigorous pursuit.

644. **c.** *Meekly* means not violent or strong; *forcefully* means powerfully.

645. **a.** *Complacent* means self-satisfied or unconcerned.

646. **b.** To be *ambiguous* is to be equivocal or obscure; to be *certain* is to be definite or fixed.

647. **a.** To *esteem* is to have favorable regard; to *disrespect* is to lack courteous regard.

648. **c.** To be *eloquent* is to be fluent; to be *inarticulate* is to be unable to speak with clarity.

649. **a.** A *deterrent* prevents or discourages; *encouragement* inspires or heartens.

650. **d.** Someone who is *impertinent* is rude; someone who is *polite* is courteous.

651. **c.** To be *ludicrous* is to be absurd; to be *reasonable* is to be rational.

652. **b.** To be *archaic* is to be ancient or outdated; to be *modern* is to be up to date.

653. **d.** *Sullen* means gloomy or dismal; *jovial* means very happy.

654. **a.** To be in *awe* of something is to admire it; to have *contempt* for something is to consider it worthless.

655. **b.** *Taut* means extremely tight; *relaxed* means not tense.

656. **a.** To *rile* is to upset; to *appease* is to pacify or satisfy.

657. **d.** To *mar* is to damage or deface; to *repair* is to restore or fix.

658. **d.** A *skeptic* is someone who doubts; a *believer* is the opposite of a skeptic.

659. **a.** To be a *predecessor* is to be one who precedes or comes before another; to be a *successor* is to be one who succeeds or comes after another.

660. **b.** To be *hypothetical* is to be suppositional or contingent on being tested; to be *actual* is to exist in fact or reality.

661. **a.** To *enhance* is to increase or augment; to *diminish* is to make smaller.

SET 34 (Page 80)

662. **d.** An *intrepid* person approaches a challenge without fear, which is the opposite of *fearful*.

663. **a.** *Methodical* means careful or in a planned manner; *erratic* means having no fixed course.

664. **d.** *Latent* means present but not active; *active* is the opposite.

665. **a.** *Affable* means pleasant and at ease; agreeable.

666. **c.** *Trepidation* means fear; the opposite would be *fearlessness*.

667. **a.** *Auspicious* means something taken as a sign of promising success; the opposite is *unpromising*.

668. **c.** *Militant* means engaged in warfare or combat; *pacifistic* means engaged in peace and diplomacy.

669. **b.** *Furtively* means done stealthily or secretively.

670. **d.** *Entice* means to attract by arousing hope; *repel* means to drive away.

671. **c.** *Ingenuous* means noble, honorable, natural, or candid; the opposite would be *calculating*.

672. **b.** To be *ostentatious* is to be showy and boastful; the opposite would be *humble*.

673. **a.** *Endorse* means to approve; *condemn* means to disapprove.

674. **c.** *Accede* means to express approval or give consent; *disapprove* means to express disapproval.

675. **b.** *Copious* means plentiful; *meager* means deficient in quality or numbers.

676. **b.** *Ambivalence* is uncertainty as to which approach to follow; *decisiveness* is having the power or quality of deciding.

677. **b.** *Divergent* means differing from a standard; *identical* means being the same.

678. **d.** *Pensive* means sadly thoughtful; thoughtless means lacking concern for others, careless, or devoid of thought.

679. **a.** One definition of *discernible* is visible with the eyes, so the opposite would be *invisible*.

680. **c.** *Vacillate* means to waver or hesitate; *resolve* means to deal with successfully.

681. **c.** *Abhor* means to regard with repugnance; *desire* means to long for or hope for.

682. **b.** *Chortle* means to laugh or chuckle; a *moan* is a low, prolonged sound of pain or grief.

683. **d.** *Raucous* means boisterous and disorderly; *calm* is the opposite.

684. **c.** *Deplete* means to lessen in quantity, content, or value; *replace* means to put something in place of.

685. **d.** *Equanimity* means evenness of mind, especially under great stress; *perplexity* means a state of bewilderment.

SET 35 (Page 83)

686. **c.** *Scarcely* is the opposite of *mostly,* and *quietly* is the opposite of *loudly.* Choices **a** and **b** are clearly not opposites of quietly. Choice **d** means the same as quietly.

687. **d.** *Candid* and *indirect* are opposing traits. *Honest* and *devious* are opposing traits. The answer is not choice **a,** because frank means the same thing as candid. Wicked (**b**) is incorrect because even though it is a negative trait, it does not mean the opposite of honest. Choice **c** is incorrect because truthful and honest mean the same thing.

688. **a.** *Meaningful* is the opposite of *insignificant.* *Essential* is the opposite of *unnecessary.* Choice **b** is incorrect because the word important has a similar meaning to essential. The answer is not choice **c** or **d** because neither is the opposite of essential.

689. **b.** *Simple* is the opposite of *complex. Trivial* is the opposite of *significant.* The answer is not choice **a** or **c** because neither of these is the opposite of trivial. Choice **d** is incorrect because irrelevant means about the same as trivial.

690. **b.** *Elated* is the opposite of *despondent; enlightened* is the opposite of *ignorant.* The answer is not choice **b** because aware is a synonym for enlightened. The answer is not choice **c** or **d** because neither of these is the opposite of enlightened.

691. **a.** *Divulge* and *conceal* are opposite in meaning. *Conform* and *differ* are antonyms. The other choices are not the opposite of conform.

692. **c.** *Admire* and *despise* are antonyms. *Praise* and *admonish* are opposite in meaning. The other choices are not the opposite of praise.

693. **d.** *Advance* and *retreat* are antonyms. *Curtail* and *prolong* are opposite in meaning. The other choices are not the opposite of curtail.

694. **a.** *Gratuitous* and *expensive* are antonyms. *Sedentary* and *active* are opposite in meaning. The other choices are not the opposite of sedentary.

695. **c.** *Gluttonous* (meaning ravenous, piggish, or greedy) and *abstemious* (meaning moderate or abstinent) are antonyms. *Complimentary* and *disparaging* are opposite in meaning. The other choices are not the opposite of complimentary.

696. **b.** *Trust* and *suspicion* are antonyms. *Apex* and *nadir* are opposite in meaning. The other choices are not the opposite of apex.

697. **a.** *Deprivation* and *affluence* are antonyms. *Capitulation* and *resistance* are opposite in meaning. The other choices are not the opposite of capitulation.

698. **c.** *Companion* and *enemy* are antonyms. *Anonymity* and *fame* are opposite in meaning. The other choices are not the opposite of anonymity.

699. **d.** *Inebriated* and *sober* are antonyms. *Atrocious* and *noble* are opposite in meaning. The other choices are not the opposite of atrocious.

700. **b.** *Ornately* and *plainly* are antonyms. *Blithely* and *morosely* are opposite in meaning. The other choices are not the opposite of blithely.

SECTION 4: SPELLING

SET 36 (Page 86)

701. **c.** belief
702. **d.** insight
703. **b.** sensitive
704. **d.** magazine
705. **a.** magic
706. **a.** prosecuted
707. **c.** conspicuous
708. **a.** shrivel
709. **b.** situation
710. **c.** clammy
711. **a.** superb
712. **b.** jealous
713. **b.** terrific
714. **d.** sheriff
715. **c.** obsession

SET 37 (Page 88)

716. **d.** jeopardy
717. **c.** magnificent
718. **b.** mechanical
719. **d.** illicit
720. **a.** inquiry
721. **a.** terminate
722. **a.** persecuted
723. **b.** peculiar
724. **d.** psychology
725. **d.** license
726. **a.** irresistible
727. **d.** parallel
728. **a.** stabilize
729. **c.** irrelevant
730. **b.** encouraging

SET 38 (Page 90)

731. **a.** commitment
732. **c.** ridiculous
733. **d.** anonymous
734. **a.** extraordinary
735. **b.** assurance
736. **a.** frequently
737. **c.** emphasis
738. **a.** delirious
739. **d.** aspiration
740. **b.** exercise
741. **c.** compatible
742. **a.** accustomed
743. **b.** commencement
744. **d.** supervisor
745. **b.** pneumonia

SET 39 (Page 92)

746. pianos
747. skies
748. mice
749. bunches
750. strawberries
751. shelves
752. boxes
753. deer
754. stimuli
755. sons-in-law
756. gases
757. industries
758. handfuls
759. tomatoes
760. crises
761. memoranda
762. species
763. antennae, or antennas

SET 40 (Page 92)

764. receive
765. piece
766. reign
767. either
768. weight
769. deceive
770. yield
771. caffeine
772. friendly
773. grief
774. efficient
775. conceited
776. achieve
777. foreign
778. variety
779. patient
780. quietly

SET 41 (Page 93)

781. c. babies
782. d. no mistakes
783. a. announcement
784. c. literature
785. b. servant
786. d. no mistakes
787. d. no mistakes
788. b. unnecessary
789. a. villain
790. a. hindrance
791. c. testimony
792. d. no mistakes
793. d. no mistakes
794. a. quantity
795. c. resistant
796. b. contradict
797. b. reversal
798. c. marshmallow
799. d. no mistakes
800. a. ravenous

SET 42 (Page 95)

801. **a.** phenomenal
802. **b.** temperature
803. **c.** athletic
804. **d.** no mistakes
805. **c.** circumference
806. **d.** no mistakes
807. **a.** poultry
808. **b.** strengthen
809. **b.** finality
810. **d.** no mistakes
811. **a.** religious
812. **d.** no mistakes
813. **b.** delinquent
814. **c.** forecast
815. **d.** no mistakes
816. **a.** righteous
817. **a.** sincerely
818. **b.** kindergarten
819. **c.** bankruptcy
820. **d.** no mistakes

SET 43 (Page 97)

821. **c.** campaign
822. **b.** respiration
823. **a.** potato
824. **b.** rehearsal
825. **c.** fascinated
826. **a.** destructive
827. **c.** dissolve
828. **d.** no mistakes
829. **b.** forfeit
830. **b.** meteorology
831. **a.** adjournment
832. **c.** vengeance
833. **c.** tremendous
834. **d.** no mistakes
835. **c.** capitalization
836. **a.** gnarled
837. **b.** parenthesis
838. **d.** no mistakes
839. **c.** sonnet
840. **a.** depot

SET 44 (Page 99)

841. **a.** prescribe
842. **b.** personnel
843. **d.** no mistakes
844. **c.** scrutiny
845. **c.** luxuriant
846. **a.** bachelor
847. **b.** gratitude
848. **d.** no mistakes
849. **a.** column
850. **b.** bulletin
851. **c.** embassy
852. **d.** no mistakes
853. **d.** no mistakes
854. **b.** questionnaire
855. **c.** zenith
856. **a.** pungent
857. **a.** wrestle
858. **c.** hygienic
859. **b.** carburetor
860. **d.** no mistakes

SET 45 (Page 101)

861. **b.** illegal
862. **a.** colossal
863. **b.** corrosive
864. **c.** tyranny
865. **d.** no mistakes
866. **a.** fatigue
867. **c.** gymnast
868. **a.** gullible
869. **b.** vacancy
870. **b.** contemptible
871. **c.** tranquil
872. **d.** no mistakes
873. **a.** traitor
874. **a.** manacle
875. **b.** volatile
876. **d.** no mistakes
877. **d.** no mistakes
878. **c.** omnivorous
879. **b.** zealotry
880. **b.** rheostat

SET 46 (Page 103)

881. b. *Dessert* is an after-dinner treat; a *desert* is arid land.

882. b. A *council* is a governing body; to *counsel* is to give advice.

883. a. *Fair* means equitable; a *fare* is a transportation fee.

884. c. *Site* refers to a place; *cite* means "to refer to"; *sight* is the ability to see.

885. c. *By* means "near to"; *bye* means good-bye; *buy* means "to purchase."

886. a. *Fourth* refers to the number four; *forth* means forward.

887. b. *Brakes* are using for stopping vehicles; *breaks* means destroys.

888. b. *Led* is the past tense of *lead*.

889. c. *There* refers to a place; *their* is the possessive of they; *they're* means "they are."

890. a. A *piece* is a portion; *peace* means quiet.

891. c. A *right* is a privilege; to *write* is to put words on paper; a *rite* is a ceremonial action.

892. b. *Stationary* means standing still; *stationery* is writing paper.

893. a. *Mussels* are marine animals; *muscles* are body tissues.

894. b. *Passed* is the past tense of pass; *past* means a time gone by.

895. b. *Reign* means royal authority; *rein* means a strap as on a horse's bridle; *rain* means precipitation.

896. a. *Lesson* is something to be learned; *lessen* means "to reduce."

897. a. *Waste* means material that is rejected during a process; the *waist* is the middle of the body.

898. b. *Freshmen* is plural; *freshman* is singular.

899. c. *Two* is a number; *to* is a preposition that refers to direction; *too* means "more than is needed," or also.

900. c. *Eminent* refers to a prominent person; *imminent* means something is about to happen; *immanent* means existing within the mind.

SET 47 (Page 105)

901. b. *Course* means path or class at school; *coarse* means rough.

902. d. All the sentences are correct.

903. a. The verb *board* means to get on an airplane; the noun *board* means a plank of wood; *bored* means uninterested.

904. c. The verb *to pore* means to read attentively; the noun *pore* means a small opening; *pour* means dispense from a container.

905. a. If someone is *vain,* he or she is excessively prideful; a *vane* is a moveable device; a *vein* is a narrow channel, like a blood vein or the vein in a leaf.

906. d. All the sentences are correct.

907. d. All the sentences are correct.

908. b. *Capital* means monetary assets and the seat of government; it also refers to letters of the alphabet; *capitol* is a government building.

909. c. To *grate* means to cause irritation; *great* means notably large or numerous.

910. b. A *plain* is an expansive area of flat, treeless country; *plain* also means characterized by simplicity; a *plane* is a tool used to smooth wood.

911. c. *Whole* means all of one thing or complete; a *hole* is an opening.

912. a. *Morale* refers to a mental condition with regard to enthusiasm; *moral* means good in character or a lesson from a story.

SET 48 (Page 106)

913. a. dissatisfied
914. d. no mistakes
915. b. pharmacy
916. c. cemetery
917. d. no mistakes
918. a. sarcasm
919. b. fragrance
920. a. inauguration
921. b. lovely
922. c. publicity
923. d. no mistakes
924. c. military
925. a. acknowledge
926. c. witnesses
927. b. fundamental
928. d. no mistakes
929. a. uniform
930. a. niece
931. d. no mistakes
932. b. immoral
933. c. traffic
934. a. elegant

SET 49 (Page 108)

935. **a.** thriftiness
936. **d.** no mistakes
937. **b.** polar
938. **b.** resemblance
939. **a.** soothe
940. **d.** no mistakes
941. **b.** quarreled
942. **a.** probably
943. **c.** pronunciation
944. **d.** no mistakes
945. **b.** principal
946. **a.** schedule
947. **c.** knowledge
948. **d.** no mistakes
949. **a.** scissors
950. **a.** embarrassed
951. **d.** no mistakes
952. **b.** management
953. **b.** neighbor
954. **c.** symmetrical
955. **d.** no mistakes
956. **c.** procedures

SET 50 (Page 111)

957. **b.** immediately
958. **c.** February
959. **a.** sensible
960. **c.** weird
961. **d.** no mistakes
962. **a.** captain
963. **a.** sophomore
964. **a.** grammar
965. **d.** no mistakes
966. **c.** unanimous
967. **c.** overrated
968. **d.** no mistakes
969. **a.** secretary
970. **b.** impeccable
971. **b.** acquaintance
972. **d.** no mistakes
973. **c.** unfortunately
974. **a.** misspelled
975. **d.** no mistakes
976. **a.** velvet
977. **b.** truly
978. **d.** no mistakes

SET 51 (Page 113)

979. a. magnificent
980. c. pamphlet
981. c. silhouette
982. b. quartet
983. c. irreparably
984. a. burglaries
985. d. no mistakes
986. b. tetanus
987. d. no mistakes
988. a. tariff
989. c. suffrage
990. a. guidance
991. b. definitely
992. d. no mistakes
993. c. murmuring
994. d. no mistakes
995. a. ignoramus
996. c. parasites
997. d. no mistakes
998. b. beleaguered
999. d. no mistakes
1000. c. financier
1001. a. renaissance

NOTES

NOTES

NOTES

NOTES

NOTES

NOTES

NOTES

NOTES

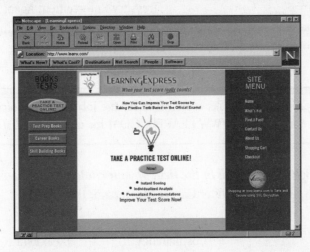

THE EXCLUSIVE LEARNINGEXPRESS ADVANTAGE—

Books Guaranteed to Improve Your Skills and Your Test Scores and Help You Succeed at School and in the Workplace.

At Last—*Test Preparation That Really Works!* Because some tests really make or break your future…

ASVAB	Postal Worker Exam
ASVAB Core Review	Federal Clerical Worker Exam
Police Officer Exam	Treasury Enforcement Agent Exam
Border Patrol Exam	Allied Health Entrance Exams
Catholic High School Entrance Exams	PPST: Praxis 1
	…and many more titles

> ***Also available:*** test preparation books customized for the job of your choice in your city/state. Call us or check out our web site WWW.LEARNX.COM for a complete list of these books.

Want a high-paying, high-demand job in the field of your choice? These books give you the detailed information you need to get ahead. We offer **Career Starters** for these fields:

Webmaster	Culinary Arts	Retailing
Paralegal	Cosmetology	Real Estate
Health Care	Teacher	EMT
Law Enforcement	Firefighter	Computer Technician
Administrative Assistant/Secretary		

Master the skills essential for success at school or at work… FAST! Quick and easy lessons to improve your reading, writing, math, and study skills *and* your on-the-job skills.

Math Essentials	Office Basics Made Easy	Reading Comprehension Success
How To Study	Job Hunting Made Easy	Writing Skills Success
Practical Spelling	Getting Organized At Work	Vocabulary & Spelling Success
Read Better, Remember More	Networking for Novices	Reasoning Skills Success
Practical Vocabulary	Effective Business Speaking	Practical Math
Improve Your Writing For Work	Technical Writing	1001 Math Problems
The Secrets of Taking Any Test	Visual Literacy	501 Reading Comprehension Questions
		…and more

And to help parents help their children succeed in school:

A Parent's Guide To Standardized Tests In School
Homework Helper 1st Grade
Homework Helper 2nd Grade

To find out more about these books, or for a complete list of LearningExpress titles, check out WWW.LEARNX.COM or call us toll-free at 1-888-551-JOBS.